Published by Tide-mark Press Ltd.
P.O. Box 20, Windsor, CT 06095-0020
In Canada: 34 Armstrong Avenue, Georgetown, Ontario L7G 4R9

Printed in Korea by Samhwa Printing Co.

Design and typography by Jane Kirk and Dan Veale

Special thanks to Lorraine Alexson for proofreading this edition and others,
and also to Robert Manning, who worked on previous editions.

Tall Ships® is a registered mark of the American Sail Training Association.

Fourth Edition — Updated and Revised

Library of Congress Control Number 2006903159

ISBN 978 159490236-9

TALL
SHIPS

By Thaddeus Koza

Published by

TIDE-MARK
PRESS

Windsor,
Connecticut

THIS BOOK IS

DEDICATED TO MY SON,

ALEXANDRE,

WHOSE SPIRIT FILLS

MORE THAN SAILS.

CONTENTS

ACKNOWLEDGMENTS

Special thanks to the photographers who supplied images of the following vessels: *Akogare* by Toshi Yamazaki; *Inland Seas,* courtesy of *Inland Seas* Education Association; *James Craig,* courtesy of Hugh Lander and the *James Craig* Foundation; *Jeanie Johnston,* courtesy of the *Jeanie Johnston* Project; *Lady Nelson,* courtesy of Irene Schaffer and the Friends of *Lady Nelson; Niagara,* courtesy of Jonathan Dickinson; *Picton Castle,* courtesy of David Marshall; *Pommern,* courtesy of Jyrki Abrahamsson; *Prince William, Stavros S Niarchos, INS Tarangini,* and *Tenacious,* courtesy of MAX Photography; *Star of India,* courtesy of Benson Lee.; *Friends Good Will,* courtesy of David Johnson; *Madeline,* courtesy of Edgar Bringman; and *Tabor Boy,* courtesy of R. Thompson.

Pam Vuckson and Capt. Tony Anderson of SALTS.

Jay Babina of Jason Designs, Branford, Connecticut

Susan Berman and her staff at the North Kingstown (Rhode Island) Public Library, who found the facts connected to the flotsam and jetsam of my mind's wanderings.

Zygmunt Choren, Choren Designs, Gdansk, Poland

Ole R. Iversen, Secretary General, Stiftelsen Skoleskipet *Christian Radich*, Oslo, Norway

Robin Krohn of the Maritime and Seafood Industry Museum of Biloxi, Mississippi, and Peg Tigue of the *Kalmar Nyckel* Foundation

Capt. Robin Snouck-Hurgronje of the *Stad Amsterdam,* and Cees Rosman, Carola Hromadka, and Henriette Sulman of the *Stad Amsterdam* office

Per Langhelle, General Manager, Stiftelsen Seilskipet *Statsraad Lehmkuhl,* Bergen, Norway

Peter Smales of the Cutty Sark Press Office, London; Steen Bjerre of the Aalborg, Denmark Press Office; Kathy Hill of the Great Chesapeake Bay Schooner Race; and Anne Burlat of Brest/Douarnenez '98.

A special thanks to the staff of the McKillop Library at Salve Regina University in Newport, Rhode Island, for their patience and direction

Rafe Parker, Paul Horowitz, Peter Mollo, and Capt. Sean Bercaw of the Sea Education Association and the *Robert C. Seamans*

Mrs. Esther Tibbs, Marketing Officer, Sail Training Association, Hampshire, United Kingdom

Lori Aguiar, Steve Baker, Peter Mello, and Capt. David Wood of the American Sail Training Association in Newport, Rhode Island

A number of captains and masters have given their time and deck space, knowledge, and hospitality to assist in the development of this book. Among the many are: Capt. Joe Davis, Capt. Emilio de Rogatis, Capt. Kip Files, Capt. Pete Hall, Capt. Jan Miles, Capt. Tadeusz Olechnowicz, Capt. Dan Quinn, Capt. Rob Ruschak, Capt. Henryk Sniegocki, and Capt. Witek Zdrojewski. And invariably, the list grows as the fleet grows and as the need for information becomes voracious.

I also thank Capt. Viktor Antonov of *Mir,* Capt. Ned Chalker, Ecuadorian Naval Attaché, Capt. Henrik Karlsson of the Maritime Museum in Marienhamn, Finland, Capt. Diego Mantilla, Capt. Dan Morehead of *Picton Castle,* Capt. Bo Rosbjerg of *Jens Krogh,* Capt. Marek Szymonski of the *Dar Mlodziezy,* and Capt. Scott Thomas of the *Highlander Seas.*

And to the "Fab Five" of Ann Arbor:
Bob, Fred, Jay, Paul, and Ross, who have provided snug harbors and sound advice for as long as the rhumb line of this passage to print has taken, and then some.

Finally, to correct an oversight in the Acknowledgments in the first edition of *Tall Ships,* a salute to R. Jonathan Meigs.
Thanks also to Alex's mom, Margaret Chapman, for the fine portrait of our son.

TALL SHIPS IN THE TWENTY-FIRST CENTURY

When we hear the words "tall ships," we conjure an image in our minds of grand ships with masts proudly reaching skyward, billowing white sails, and a spiderweb of lines and rigging extending in every direction. To describe them, we use words that regularly do not find themselves together: beautiful, powerful, quiet, fast, efficient, graceful, romantic, courageous, majestic, resourceful. They are awe-inspiring and dream-inducing. They cast upon us a sense of nostalgia, history, and simpler times.

Sailing ships have played several important roles throughout the course of history. They have helped us prove the world was not flat, explore oceans, discover distant lands, defend shores from aggressors, extend national boundaries, carry immigrants to new countries, harvest the seas, and bring exotic cargo home.

Thankfully, as the photographs in the following pages attest, tall ships are alive and well in our modern world. They sail our lakes, bays, seas, and oceans, fulfilling a wide variety of occupations including naval sail trainers, economic ambassadors, historical presenters, adventure vacation cruisers, scientific researchers, and sea educators. Every year new tall ships join the world's fleet in an amazing variety of rigs, sizes, and missions.

The tall ships renaissance started in the mid-1950s when London solicitor Bernard Morgan and several European colleagues launched the idea of bringing together what they imagined to be the last of the grand square riggers for a race celebrating the end of the Age of Sail. Closer to home, Barclay Warburton III of Newport, Rhode Island, recognized the incredible power that the sea and sailing ships had to positively influence the lives of young Americans. He had the vision and leadership to establish the American Sail Training Association in 1973. These gentlemen, and many, many others who have followed in their footsteps, have provided unique and powerful educational opportunities for millions of young people across the globe, and have given the public the chance to view these inspiring vessels up close and renew our connection to the sea. Sail training races and tall ship port festivals bring together people from many different seafaring nations and advance cultural exchange and international goodwill that is so important in the world today.

From our perspective at the American Sail Training Association, the real power of a tall ship is its nearly unparalleled ability to teach. We learn most effectively through experiences, and life at sea offers plenty of opportunity. Sail training is not learning to sail, but rather learning through sailing. In modern times there are few genuine opportunities to explore new worlds and challenge oneself; sail training offers such opportunities. Sail training builds self-reliance and, at the same time, an appreciation for the benefits and necessity of teamwork onboard ship. It fosters respect for the sea, the environment, the ship, shipmates, and self.

It is often stated that young people between the ages of 15 and 25 are the primary beneficiaries of traditional sail training: that is, living aboard a sailing ship for an extended period in a summer camplike experience. But we like to say that sail training experiences are valuable for "youth of all ages" and voyages of any duration and distance. A middle school student on a field trip for the day, a college junior away for a semester at sea, a couple celebrating an anniversary on an adventure-travel sailing expedition, a family on a weekend excursion on a Maine windjammer, older adults on an Elderhostel Adventures Afloat program: these are just some of the diverse opportunities available to sail aboard these beautiful tall ships and to create memories that will last for a lifetime.

So the next time you see a tall ship sailing on the horizon or docked in port, stop dreaming about the past. Remember that tall ships like those on the following pages offer incredible adventure and educational experiences today. So grab your duffle bag and embark on your own voyage of discovery!

Peter A. Mello
Executive Director
American Sail Training Association
www.tallships.sailtraining.org

The mission of the American Sail Training Association is to encourage character building through sail training, to promote sail training to the North American public, and to support education under sail.

PREFACE

In the opening years of this century, the fleet of tall ships endured the same critical factors as the world in general: global warming and financial cooling. While tall ships gain in popularity and the fleet increases, the difficulties of maintaining vessels and crews have multiplied. Several vessels have faded due to economic shortfall and others encountered rogue weather—perhaps the effects of ecological change.

Both history and Hollywood have benefited some. The movies *Master and Commander* and *Pirates of the Caribbean* (with its sequels) have employed several vessels in their productions and thus, brought monetary stability to the upkeep and maintenance of several vessels. HMS *Rose* has become the HMS *Surprise*, and relocated to San Diego, California as a consequence of her participation in the Patrick O'Brian adaptation. *Californian*, *Lady Washington*, *Bounty*, and *Providence* were employed in the filming of the original *Pirates* film and its sequels.

New vessels have been launched and planned, with Sweden producing two interesting projects: the *Götheborg* project to create a replica of a seventeenth-century East Indiaman, and the Stockholm brig, *Tre Kronor*. The latter, launched in 2005, will be sailing in Stockholm by the end of 2006. On the American side, schooners have been built in Virginia and South Carolina, and the eastern shore of Maryland has added *Sultana* to the fleet.

The weather has taken its toll on several important tall ships. On October 21, 2004, the typhoon *Tokage* caught the *Kaiwo Maru II*, seriously damaging the rig and hull. It has taken over a year of re-riggings and structural repairs to return her to service. An un-charted sandbar caused the grounding of the new *Irving Johnston* off of Oxnard, California, in March 2005, causing serious water damage. In September 2005, while racing from Torbay to Santander, Spain, the *Pride Of Baltimore II* encountered gale winds, and tumultuous seas in the Bay of Biscay and was de-masted. It has taken 6 months and a half million dollars to restore her. She is expected to return to North America at press time.

In addition, several ships changed owners and ports. The *Hawaiian Chieftain* left San Francisco Bay to the east coast, and then back to the Pacific and a new home and mission in Westport, WA. The *Westward* also went from Cape Cod and S.E.A. to the farther horizons of the Ocean Classroom Foundation and a home port in Maine. Lastly, the *Tree of Life* was sold and moved to Vancouver, BC.

The fleet of tall ships continues to evolve and to explore the ever-changing horizons and domains of the "ocean-planet." With ever-increasing audiences and the support of harbors large and small, the ships bring romance, adventure, and international friendship along with sail training.

Thaddeus Koza
1 March 2006

TALL SHIP RIGS

FULL-RIGGED SHIP
Three or more masts, all square-rigged

BARQUE
Three or more masts, all square-rigged except the
aftermast, which is fore-and-aft rigged

BRIG
Two masts, both square-rigged

BARQUENTINE
Three or more masts, all fore-and-aft rigged except the
foremast, which is fully square-rigged

BRIGANTINE
Two masts, the foremast is fully square-rigged
and the mainmast is fore-and-aft rigged

TOPSAIL SCHOONER
Two or more masts, the foremast carries
square-rigged sails over fore-and-aft sails

SCHOONER
Two or more masts, fore-and-aft rigged

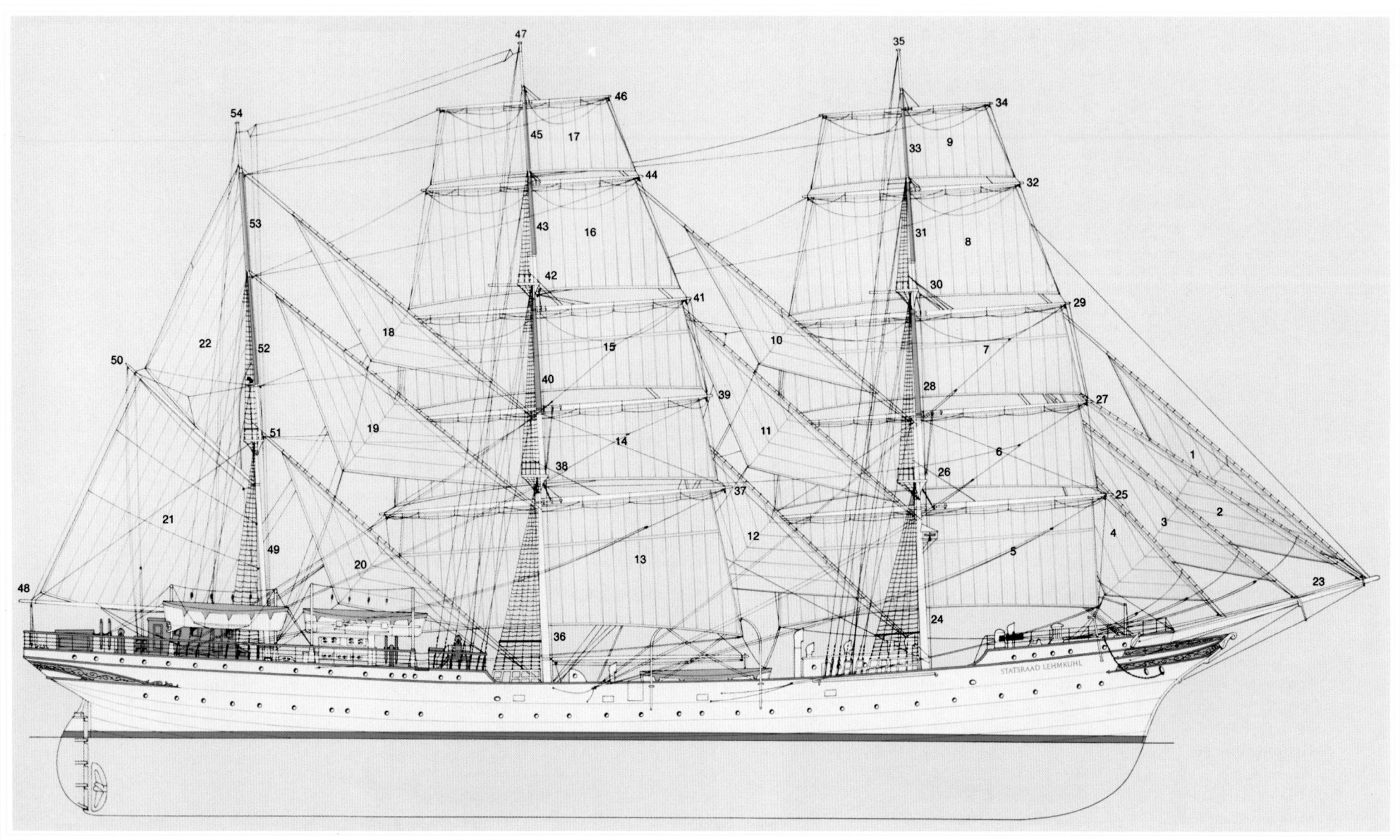

THE RIG AND SAIL PLAN OF STATSRAAD LEHMKUHL

Norway's largest and oldest sailing ship, *Statsraad Lehmkuhl*, has a displacement of 1701 gross tons. She has a sail area of 2026 square meters (21,800 square feet) distributed among 22 sails. The addition of modern accommodations reduced the ship's capacity for trainees from 200 to 150. There are cabins for the regular crew of 20. An 1125 h.p. diesel engine is capable of moving the ship at up to 11 knots in fair weather.

In consideration of the cadets' security, *Statsraad Lehmkuhl* was originally given a reduced rig relative to its size. Altough this is a handicap when racing with other Class A vessels in light wind, the ship sails well in more robust conditions.

The accompanying illustration is provided through the courtesy of Stiftelsen Seilskipet Statsraad Lehmkuhl, Holmedalsgården, Bryggen, N5003, Bergen, Norway.

SAILS

1 Flying jib
2 Outer jib
3 Inner jib
4 Fore topmast staysail
5 Fore course sail
6 Fore lower topsail
7 Fore upper topsail
8 Fore topgallant sail
9 Fore royal
10 Main royal staysail
11 Main topgallant staysail
12 Main topmast staysail
13 Main course sail
14 Main lower topsail
15 Main upper topsail
16 Main topgallant sail
17 Main royal
18 Mizzen topgallant staysail
19 Mizzen topmast staysail
20 Mizzen staysail
21 Mizzen
22 Mizzen gaff-topsail

MASTS AND YARDS

23 Bowsprit
24 Fore mast
25 Fore yard
26 Fore lower cross-trees
27 Fore lower topsail yard
28 Fore topmast
29 Fore upper topsail yard
30 Fore topmast cross-trees
31 Fore topgallant mast
32 Fore topgallant yard
33 Fore royal mast
34 Fore royal yard
35 Fore masthead
36 Main mast
37 Main yard
38 Main lower cross-trees
39 Main lower topsail yard
40 Main topmast
41 Main upper topsail yard
42 Main topmast cross-trees
43 Main topgallant mast
44 Main topgallant yard
45 Main royal mast
46 Main royal yard
47 Main masthead
48 Spanker boom
49 Mizzenmast
50 Spanker gaff
51 Mizzen cross-trees
52 Mizzen topmast
53 Mizzen topgallant mast
54 Mizzen masthead

CLASSES OF TALL SHIPS

As tall ships travel around the world, they frequently race with one another from port to port. Since hull length is a major determinant of speed through the water, these vessels have been grouped into classes to keep the competition fair.

Class A includes all square-rigged vessels over 120 feet (36.6m) in length overall, as well as fore-and-aft rigged vessels of 160 feet (48.8m) or more in length overall.

Class A, Division II, covers all square-rigged vessels (including ships, barques, barquentines, brigs, and brigantines) less than 120 feet (36.6m) in overall length.

Class B includes fore-and-aft rigged vessels (topsail schooners, schooners, ketches, yawls, cutters, and sloops) of between 160 feet (48.8m) and 120 feet (36.6m) long overall.

Class C covers all other fore-and-aft rigged vessels with a waterline length of at least 30 feet (9.14m) in three divisions. Division I covers all gaff-rigged vessels of less than 100 feet (30.5m) not racing with spinnakers and all vessels built before 1939 not already included in Classes A, AII, and B. Division II includes all Bermudian-rigged vessels of less than 100 feet overall not racing with spinnakers. Division III covers all vessels of less than 100 feet (30.5m) long overall racing with spinnakers.

Note that length overall is the length between the forward end of the stem post and the after end of the stern post. It does not include the bowsprit, pulpit, or any other extension at the bow or stern.

Pictured here are three different classes of tall ships. The largest of the three is *Sagres II* (with white sails), a Class A. *Roseway* is a Class B and carries tanbark sails. The smallest vessel and a Class C is the Polish sloop *Smuga Ciena*.

Together, four of the largest tall ships in the world measure more than a quarter of a mile from stem to stern. They are (left to right) *Kruzenshtern* at 376 feet, *Esmeralda* at 371 feet, *Sedov* at 386 feet, and *Libertad* at 356 feet.

TALL SHIPS, TALL SHIPS!

With ships the sea was sprinkled far and nigh,
Like stars in heaven, and joyously it showed;
Some lying fast at anchor in the road,
Some veering up and down, one knew not why.
A goodly Vessel did I then espy
Come like a giant from a haven broad;
And lustily along the bay she strode,
Her tackling rich, and of apparel high.
This Ship was nought to me, nor I to her,
Yet I pursued her with a Lover's look;
This Ship to all the rest did I prefer:
When will she turn, and whither? She will brook
No tarrying; where She comes the winds must stir:
On went She, and due north her journey took.

—William Wordsworth, 1806

The initial years of the twenty-first century have seen the construction of a number of new tall ships: the two sister clippers; *Stad Amsterdam* of the Netherlands and *Cisne Branco* of Brazil; the Great Lakes schooner *Denis Sullivan;* the oceanographic American brigantine *Robert C. Seamans;* the British Columbian schooner *Pacific Swift;* and the packet barque *Jeanie Johnston* of Ireland. These vessels, along with a series of tall ships that are currently in the works, including *Sultana, Lynx,* and the twin brigantines *Irving Johnson* and *Exy Johnson* of the Los Angeles Maritime Institute, all speak to the success of existing sail training programs around the world and reinforce the need to continue the application of the ideals that sustain sail training programs.

During the second half of the twentieth century, the purpose of the tall ships was to serve as educational platforms to prepare young trainees in maritime countries for future careers in naval or merchant marine services. Now, as new vessels and rigs proliferate, specific tall ship programs have been defined in the fields of ecological and environmental sciences, as well as in the more generic programs of adventure and discovery. A mandate has been set to enlighten the seas with global understanding and peace. As new programs and projects emerge, it is apparent that the intrinsic goals and ideals of sail training have a lasting value and a more prescient function in the ever-tightening globe we call Earth.

Despite the artificial boundaries that all navigators, sailors, and explorers must understand in order to cross the waters of the world, these vessels serve to break barriers and to widen the perspectives of those whom they serve and visit. The tall ships are indeed goodwill ambassadors that bring national pride, cultural values, and humane ideals to the ports and nations on which they call. Tolerance and understanding are but a hallmark of tall ship crew exchanges.

The year 2001 saw a number of benchmark moments in the mission of tall ship crews to promote worldwide goodwill and understanding. In August 2001, *Shabab of Oman* of the Sultanate of Oman won the Cutty Sark Trophy, a designation awarded by the ships' captains who participate in the annual Cutty Sark Tall Ship Races to honor the crew that has contributed the most toward international friendship and understanding. It was the third time that the wooden-hulled barquentine from Oman won the trophy.

Also in 2001, two of the primary planners of tall ships, Rafe Parker of the Sea Education Association of Woods Hole, Massachusetts, and Capt. David Wood, former chair of the American Sail Training Association (ASTA), spoke of the need for the continuation of sail training in today's complex world.

The crew of *Shabab of Oman*

Christian Radich

At the dedication of the new brigantine *Robert C. Seamans* in Tacoma, Washington, in July, Rafe Parker spoke of the "value-laden lessons" to be taught by tall ships in the matriculation of young trainees. He spoke of the "endurance, the compassion, the courage, the accountability, the sense of awe, the trust, and the humility" to be learned by a cadet or student in days crewing on a long sea voyage.

The endurance of the duty to watch, the endurance of a commitment to goals, the compassion for fellow crew members and former sailors, the courage to perform duties and to take risks, the accountability of one's actions on deck with the crew and the ship or on shore, the sense of awe at completing a common task 100 feet above the water or on deck and witnessing the exuberant and ferocious sea or a calm, color-saturated sunset, and the humility of having one's aspirations delayed or denied by forces of nature, accident, or fate are the experiences defined and determined in the life of tall ships.

Lastly, Rafe Parker discussed the lesson of "an interdependence with all things, on a global level, with each other, and within ourselves. Acknowledging that we cannot exist on this planet, nor successfully survive six weeks aboard a tall ship, without fully accepting this vital condition—interdependence."

Capt. David Wood evoked a similar tone and response in addressing a group of journalists and the membership of ASTA when he delineated these same commitments:

"Sail training brings people together in a challenging situation and forces them to summon all their resources to meet difficulty and danger alongside others they may not know at all, but with whom they share a common goal and a unique mutual interdependence. Tall ship events bring proud and substantial symbols of other places and cultures, crewed by enthusiastic representatives of those places and cultures, to port cities, where they mingle in an atmosphere of friendship and celebration of both their differences and similarities."

Sail training, and ASTA's TALL SHIPS CHALLENGE®, will be only a small part of the coming effort to bridge the gulf that opened before us on September 11, 2001. That effort will take years and require the efforts of millions of people around the world. As elements of the global effort to bring people together so that hatred and violence can be diminished in the world, they constitute an undertaking that now seems more important than ever.

Stad Amsterdam

THE
TALL
SHIPS

A.J. MEERWALD

The gaff schooner *A.J. Meerwald* was built as an oyster dredger in 1928. Designed for the waters of Delaware Bay, her shallow 6-foot 3-inch draft reflects the locale and the work for which she was intended.

Augustus Joseph Meerwald, who ordered her construction at the Charles H. Stolman & Sons Shipyard, was a successful oysterman from South Dennis, New Jersey, and already owned two other vessels. Unfortunately, *A.J. Meerwald* seemed doubly plagued: She shared the bitter fruits of the Great Depression and then the infertility of the Delaware Bay oyster beds. Her business failed, but she endured.

During World War II, *A.J. Meerwald* served as a fireboat on Delaware Bay. After the war, she fell into disrepair and was almost lost until the energetic Delaware Bay Schooner Project began her restoration in 1988. After nearly a decade of care and work, she was put into service in 1996 and in 1998 designated New Jersey's official tall ship.

A.J. Meerwald offers environmental and educational services to schools, as well as a public sail program for interested adults. Her home port is the historic town of Bivalve on the Maurice River in southern New Jersey.

SCANTLINGS
Length overall: 115'
Beam: 22' 1"
Draft: 6' 3"
Hull: Wood
Rig: Gaff schooner
Year built: 1928
Home port: Bivalve, New Jersey
Flag: United States

SCANTLINGS
Length overall: 135'
Beam: 21'
Draft: 12'
Hull: Wood
Rig: Gaff topsail schooner
Year built: 1913
Home port: Port Townsend, Washington
Flag: United States

ADVENTURESS

Commissioned originally as a private yacht to gather Arctic specimens, *Adventuress* was built in 1913 at the Rice Brothers shipyard in East Boothbay, Maine. After her maiden voyage around Cape Horn to the Bering Sea by the Straits of Magellan, *Adventuress* was acquired by Bar Pilots of San Francisco Bay, where she served until 1952.

In 1960, "Doc" Freeman of the Lake Union Chandlery in Seattle brought her to Washington's Puget Sound. Two years later Ernestine Bennett and a group of Girl Scouts seeking a challenge discovered *Adventuress*. Mrs. Bennett became the helmswoman for a number of programs and ownership changes that led to the floating classroom program now known as Sound Experience.

Under the auspices of Sound Experience, each year *Adventuress* offers more than four thousand young people a variety of programs that explore the environmental and ecological concerns of Puget Sound.

Restored to her original elegant profile and accorded National Historic Landmark status, *Adventuress* is referred to admiringly as Queen of the Sound, which can only please her designer, B.B. Crowningshield.

AKOGARE

Built by the city of Osaka, Japan, as a good-will ambassador for the municipality, *Akogare* is the latest vessel to join the expanding Japanese sail training fleet. Her name means "the yearning," and she is a topsail schooner that began sailing and training programs in 1994.

SCANTLINGS
Length overall: 171'
Beam: 28' 6"
Draft: 13'
Hull: Steel
Rig: Topsail schooner
Year built: 1993
Home port: Osaka, Japan
Flag: Japan

ALABAMA

A former pilot schooner, *Alabama* was originally built for the Mobile Bar Pilot Association of Pensacola, Florida, in 1926.
She is a fine example of the Gloucester fishing schooners that worked off Cape Ann in the early 1900s.

Restored by Capt. Robert Douglas and the G. S. Maynard Shipbuilding Company of Vineyard Haven, Massachusetts, between
1995 and 1998, this schooner is one of two vessels offering day sails along the New England coast for the Coastwise Packet Company.

SCANTLINGS
Length overall: 120'
Beam: 21'
Draft: 12' 6"
Hull: Wood
Rig: Schooner
Year built: 1926
Home port: Vineyard
   Haven, Massachusetts
Flag: United States

ALBANUS

Rigged as a galleass, *Albanus* carries a Finnish variant of the traditional ketch rig.

The original *Albanus* was built in 1904 by one of the Åland Islands' most famous shipwrights, August Henriksson. Until she ran aground in 1929, *Albanus* carried firewood, agricultural products, fish, and mercantile goods to and from ports on the northern end of the Baltic, including Alan, Stockholm, Turku, Helsinki, and Reval.

During the mid-1800s, more than 300 galleasses were built in Åland. In 1986, the Albanus Ship Society was formed with the purpose of commemorating this history. The group set to work designing a rig to provide the region with a beautiful memento of its past and a living symbol of its maritime legacy.

After creating a design based on original drawings from the nineteenth century, *Albanus* took two years to build and was launched in 1988. Her rig was completed in the spring of 1989, and she first sailed in May 1989. *Albanus's* mission is to provide sail training for the youth of Mariehamn and the Åland Islands.

SCANTLINGS
Length overall: 98' 6"
Beam: 20' 3"
Draft: 6' 3"
Hull: Wood
Rig: Galleass
Year built: 1988
Home port: Mariehamn, Finland
Flag: Finland

SCANTLINGS
Length overall: 205'
Beam: 26'
Draft: 15' 6"
Hull: Steel
Rig: Barque
Year built: 1906;
   converted, 1986
Home port: Bremerhaven,
   Germany
Flag: Germany

ALEXANDER von HUMBOLDT

Outfitted in distinctive green sails, *Alexander von Humboldt* is the flagship of the Sail Training Association of Germany (STAG). Originally operated as the lightship *Kiel,* she maintained her position in the Baltic for eighty years. Retiring in 1986, she underwent extensive refitting and conversion under the supervision of Polish naval architect Zygmunt Choren.

Lightships occupy a fixed position at sea. They are outfitted with navigational lighting and sound devices to warn other ships of their position. Because of their strong hull construction, lightships are good candidates for conversion to sail. During that process the interior is rebuilt and running rigging and spars are added, along with auxiliary engines. (See also entries for *Atlantis, Den Store Bjørn,* and *Europa.*)

As the sail training vessel of STAG, *Alexander von Humboldt* now visits ports around the world as a goodwill ambassador, especially for young people with an interest in science.

The ship is named for the German scientist, traveler, and statesman Alexander von Humboldt, 1769–1859, who was also the founder of Berlin University. Von Humboldt explored South America from 1799 to 1804. His interest in isothermal conditions and the weather led him to devise a systematic strategy for agricultural development. In honor of his contributions to the understanding of the ocean and its ecology, the South Pacific's Humboldt Current was named for him.

ALMA

The last of a vanishing breed, *Alma* is a "scow" schooner. A fleet of some four hundred of these vessels carried cargo between the river towns and delta waterways connected to San Francisco Bay. Characterized by a shallow draft and wide beam, scow schooners were designed to transport such bulk cargoes as hay and grain from river shores to larger ports along the bay.

Built in 1891, *Alma* has survived more than a century on the water. She was restored and refurbished by the San Francisco Maritime National Historic Park and is docked at Hyde Street Pier near Fisherman's Wharf in San Francisco. Supported by the National Maritime Museum Association, *Alma* sails each year from March to November. Her many programs introduce trainees and apprentices to traditional sailing and wooden-boat maintenance. Her voyages also provide opportunities to learn about marine science and the ecology of San Francisco Bay.

SCANTLINGS
Length overall: 88'
Beam: 23' 6"
Draft: 3' 6"
Hull: Wood
Rig: Schooner
Year built: 1891
Home port: San Francisco, California
Flag: United States

AMERICA

Presenting a striking profile with notably raked masts, this black-hulled schooner sustains the tradition of speed, elegance, and innovation established by her namesake. She is a re-creation of the most famous racing yacht in history, the schooner *America*, which won the 100-guinea cup, now known as America's Cup, in 1851. Constructed with the assistance of fifteen major marine product manufacturers, she was built from the waterline up to replicate the lines and design of the original. *America*'s 139-foot wood-and-epoxy composite hull was completed in the fall of 1995 by Scarano Boat Building of Albany, New York.

Traveling throughout the world to demonstrate the best and most innovative products of the National Marine Manufacturing Association, *America* will sail the seven seas and maintain an aggressive travel schedule, averaging more than 20,000 miles annually.

SCANTLINGS
Length overall: 139'
Beam: 25'
Draft: 10'
Hull: Wood
Rig: Schooner
Year built: 1995
Home port: Alexandria,
  Virginia
Flag: United States

AMERICAN EAGLE

In 1984, after fifty-three years of hard fishing in the Atlantic, *American Eagle* underwent a major reconstruction at the North End Shipyard in Camden, Maine. Local stands of white pine, locust, and oak were used for her solid timber reconstruction. Thanks to the ingenuity and expertise of six schooner captains, *American Eagle* returned to the sea, joining the Maine schooner fleet.

She is now designated a national historic landmark. Her fair lines and tarred rigging bring back memories of her launch three generations ago. Today, with varnished interior cabins, an all-weather rig, and contemporary safety features, *American Eagle* is seaworthy, fast, and outfitted for comfort and convenience.

SCANTLINGS
Length overall: 121'
Beam: 20'
Draft: 11' 6"
Hull: Wood
Rig: Schooner
Year built: 1930
Home port: Rockland, Maine
Flag: United States

AMERICAN PRIDE

Built in 1941 at the Muller Boat Works in Brooklyn, New York, *American Pride* was designed as a two-masted "schooner dragger." She spent forty years working the Grand Banks and the Georges Bank fishing grounds in the Atlantic.

In January 1986 *American Pride* underwent a major overhaul. Re-rigged as a three-masted schooner, she was renamed *Natalie Todd* and joined the Maine Windjammer Fleet. In October 1996 she was purchased by the American Heritage Marine Institute and began an extended voyage through the Panama Canal to her new home in southern California. She now participates in tall ship events and supports a modest sail training and educational program for young people.

SCANTLINGS
Length overall: 129'
Beam: 21'
Draft: 10'
Hull: Wood
Rig: Schooner
Year built: 1941
Home port: Alamitos Bay, California
Flag: United States

SCANTLINGS
Length overall: 135'
Beam: 24'
Draft: 9'
Hull: Steel
Rig: Topsail schooner
Year built: 1986
Home port: Norfolk, Virginia
Flag: United States

AMERICAN ROVER

With a colorful green-and-white hull and tanbark sails, *American Rover* is easy to spot when she appears
at regattas and other events, like the Great Chesapeake Bay Schooner Race. She has an extensive day-sail
schedule out of her home port, in addition to educational field trips for students.

AMERIGO VESPUCCI

The pride of the Italian navy, *Amerigo Vespucci* conjures up memories of men-of-war from two centuries ago. Riding high in the water, with triple decks indicated by painted stripes, *Amerigo Vespucci* is a gracious twentieth-century goodwill ambassador, as well as a symbol of Italy's global maritime heritage and tradition.

Named for the great explorer and cartographer of the seventeenth century, this elegant, full-rigged ship is a grand visitor to many ceremonial parades of sail. Since her launch, *Amerigo Vespucci* has been used to train junior officers of the Italian navy.

SCANTLINGS
Length overall: 330'
Beam: 50' 9"
Draft: 23' 6"
Hull: Steel
Rig: Ship
Year built: 1931
Home port: La Spezia, Italy
Flag: Italy

AMISTAD

In 1839 the slavery trade was at its height, and ships carrying natives to the New World were arriving on a regular basis. On one particular voyage, a slave from Sierra Leone named Sengbe Pieb, and known as Cinque led a mutiny to free himself and other captives onboard the cargo schooner *La Amistad*. The story of the slavery, rebellion, and freedom that occurred that day has been immortalized in books and a movie. When John Adams, the second president of the United States, stood up as an advocate for the captives before the U.S. Supreme Court in 1841, the *Amistad* incident became a symbol of the country's idealism, struggle for racial equality, and constitutional boundaries.

To commemorate this event and its significance, the state of Connecticut, Mystic Seaport, and the Amistad America consortium built a replica of *Amistad* using traditional materials and the skilled artisans of the Mystic Seaport Museum. The low, black-hulled schooner was launched in 2000, and her maiden voyage included the tall ship events of Operation Sail 2000 in New York City.

Since that time, *Amistad* has been engaged in an extensive sailing and educational program along the Atlantic seaboard. The ship plans to cruise to the west coast of the United States to promote the idealism of its liberated sailors.

SCANTLINGS
Length overall: 129'
Beam: 22' 4"
Draft: 10' 2"
Hull: Wood
Rig: Topsail schooner
Year built: 1998–2000
Home port: New Haven, Connecticut
Flag: United States

ANGELE ALINE

Built according to one of the traditional fishing vessel designs of the northern coast of France, *Angele Aline* is actually a dundée, or ketch-rigged vessel, with a retractable bowsprit that allows extra maneuverability in channels and inlets. At the turn of the century a small fleet of such dundées was based in the old fishing village of Fécamp, on the northern coast of France. *Angele Aline* was part of that fishing fleet for ten years. She fished Scottish waters for herring and, later in the season, the sea off Normandy. Eventually she was sold to a Belgian shipbuilder. During World War II she was requisitioned by the French navy as part of the evacuation of British troops at Dunkirk. *Angele Aline* now proudly displays a commemorative plaque that identifies her as part of the fleet of Dunkirk Little Ships.

In the early 1980s she was purchased by George and Muriel Thurstan, who refitted and restored her. She remains a private vessel in charter service. For the past decade she has participated in tall ship gatherings on both sides of the Atlantic.

SCANTLINGS
Length overall: 79'
Beam: 16' 5"
Draft: 9'
Hull: Wood
Rig: Ketch
Year built: 1921
Home port: London, England
Flag: United Kingdom

SCANTLINGS
Length overall: 130'
Beam: 24'
Draft: 11'
Hull: Steel
Rig: Ketch
Year built: 1980
Home port: Camden, Maine
Flag: United States

ANGELIQUE

Designed specifically to serve the tourist trade as a windjammer, *Angelique* is ketch-rigged and built to be swift, comfortable, and safe. With her tanbark sails and a mainmast that rises 100 feet above deck, *Angelique* is a familiar sight along the "Down East" coast of Maine. With all her sails set before the wind she recalls the nineteenth-century trawlers of the North Sea and English Channel.

ANTIGUA

The three-masted *Antigua* is not a new vessel. She was converted from a deepsea trawler. Acquired by the Holland's Glorie charter group of Rotterdam, the Netherlands, she underwent an extended refitting and conversion from 1993 to 1995 and emerged as a three-masted barquentine. With sixteen cabins, *Antigua* can accommodate up to thirty-two passengers for charters or sail training.

SCANTLINGS
Length overall: 158'
Beam: 24'
Draft: 11'
Hull: Steel
Rig: Barquentine
Year built: 1956
Home port: Rotterdam
Flag: The Netherlands

SCANTLINGS
Length overall: 102'
Beam: 21' 6''
Draft: 6' 6''
Hull: Steel
Rig: Brig
Year built: 1994
Home port: Stavoren
Flag: The Netherlands

APHRODITE

Construction of this trim brig was completed in 1993. Named for the mythological
goddess of beauty and love, in Greek Aphrodite means "foam-born" or sprung from
the sea. Today's *Aphrodite* provides private charter service in Dutch waters.

APPLEDORE IV

The steel-hulled schooner *Appledore IV* was built in 1989 and purchased eight years later by the newly created, Michigan-based nonprofit group BaySail. She arrived in Bay City, Michigan, in 1998 and today plays a vital role in BaySail's mission to foster environmental stewardship of the Saginaw Bay Watershed and the Great Lakes ecosystem.

In the mid- to late-1800s, schooners were the most common vessels on the Great Lakes, used to transport lumber and other goods throughout the north country. *Appledore IV* commemorates Michigan's long maritime history through educational and sail training programs.

SCANTLINGS
Length overall: 85'
Beam: 18' 5"
Draft: 8' 6"
Hull: Steel
Rig: Topsail schooner
Year built: 1989
Home port: Bay City, Michigan
Flag: United States

ARGUS

Constructed about 1905 in Marstal, Denmark, Argus carried goods to ports on the Baltic Sea. In addition to lumber and cement, it is likely that the ship sailed to Greenland with grain and other goods, carried Greenland's salted fish to Spain, and then turned north with spices from Spain's trade with Africa and the Near East. Argus was originally operated by a family of two or three, along with a young apprentice working as a deckhand.

During World War II, Argus was pressed into German naval service and, along with guns, saw the addition of a diesel engine.

After the war, Argus continued to work until her purchase by American Tucker Thompson in 1969. He sailed Argus to Newport Beach, California, where he planned to refit her as a pleasure craft. Plans changed and she was offered for sale instead.

The Orange Empire Area Boy Scout Council purchased Argus in 1970 and since then she has sailed from Newport Beach encouraging young scouts to learn about seamanship, teamwork, and life at sea.

SCANTLINGS
Length overall: 68'
Beam: 18'
Draft: 8'
Rig: Topsail ketch
Hull: Wood
Year built: 1905
Home port: Newport
  Beach, California
Flag; United States

ARTEMIS

Named for the Greek goddess of the hunt, *Artemis* was built in Norway in 1926 and sailed for two decades as a whaling ship. Fitted with a steam engine, two auxiliary masts, and harpoon guns, she sailed out of Oslo, Norway, to hunt in the north and south polar oceans and the Bering Sea. *Artemis* was refitted in the 1950s to haul cargo between Asia and South America as a tramp freighter. Eventually sold to a Danish captain, *Artemis* continued to carry freight until the late 1990s, when her modest size made her economically impractical. She was then sold and converted in 2001 into an elegant sailing ship and now carries passengers on excursions on northern European waters.

SCANTLINGS
Length overall: 193' 6"
Beam: 23'
Draft: 11' 6"
Rig: Barque
Hull: Steel
Year built: 1926; rebuilt 2001
Home port: Franeker
Flag: The Netherlands

SCANTLINGS
Length overall: 129'
Beam: 22'
Draft: 9'
Hull: Steel
Rig: Schooner
Year built: 1991
Home port: Jakarta,
    Indonesia
Flag: Indonesia

ARUNG SAMUDERA

In 1995 the Indonesian government heralded the golden anniversary of its independence by hosting a conference, Arung Samudera '95, to draw attention to the archipelago nation. At the conclusion of the conference, a 129-foot staysail schooner purchased in New Zealand was commissioned as Indonesia's first sail training ship. Known originally as *Adventurer*, the schooner was built in 1991 to serve as a sail training vessel based in Auckland, New Zealand.

She was renamed Kri *Arung Samudera* to reflect her new home and service. The honorific "kri" is used just as "HMS" is used in Britain to designate a ship in service of the Royal Navy. Together the words "arung" and "samudera" in this context mean "cruise the ocean," a fitting goal for this adventurous schooner. *Arung Samudera* embarked on a circumnavigation of the globe as her first assignment.

ASGARD II

Asgard II upholds Ireland's proud and heroic maritime tradition. The original *Asgard* was owned and commanded by the Irish patriot Robert Erskine Childers (1870–1922). Childers was the author of the fabled novel, *Riddle of the Sands* (1903) and, as an accomplished sailor, was said to have smuggled guns aboard *Asgard* for the nationalist cause. Childers received the boat as a wedding present from Dr. Hamilton Osgood of Boston, Massachusetts, the father of his bride, Molly. The vessel's design was based on the work of Norwegian naval architect Colin Archer, whose ships were famous for their speed and maneuverability. The name *Asgard* comes from Norse legend and means "home of the gods," or the Elysian fields, the place of rest after death for the blessed.

The original vessel was purchased in 1964 by Coiste An Asgard, the Irish sail training organization, and preserved as an historic vessel. Found to be unseaworthy in 1974, she was transferred in 1979 to her now-permanent dryland berth, the Kilmainham Jail Historical Museum near Dublin.

Asgard II has been involved in full-time sail training since her launch in 1981. She too carries an historic Irish connection. Her figurehead is an effigy of Gráinne Mhoal, "Grace of the cropped hair," a legendary sixteenth-century Irish female sea captain and, some say, pirate. Also known as Grace O'Malley, this legendary figure purportedly found the gates of Castle Howth shut, kidnapped the heir to the castle in retaliation, and returned him only on condition that the gates never be locked at dinnertime and that a place always be laid for her at the table.

SCANTLINGS
Length overall: 104'
Beam: 21'
Draft: 9' 6"
Hull: Wood
Rig: Brigantine
Year built: 1981
Home port: Dublin
Flag: Ireland

TS ASTRID

The renaissance of TS *Astrid* may be more interesting than the story of her working career. Built in 1918 as a working schooner in the Netherlands, she was sold to a Swedish farmer in 1937 and carried barley, wheat, and rape seed along the Swedish coast. During World War II, she traded timber and coal between Sweden and Poland. Somehow *Astrid* came to fly the Lebanese flag in 1976, and a year later she was suspected of drug trafficking.

With British Customs close on her wake, she was abandoned by her crew and set afire, leaving only two bodies and her bare iron hull behind. Towed to Newhaven, the river Hamble seemed *Astrid*'s likely grave until Englishman Graham Neilson used his naval retirement bonus for her purchase.

The *Astrid* Trust was established in 1985 and, after four years of work, *Astrid* was rebuilt to serve as a sail training ship. By 1997 financial setbacks led to *Astrid*'s sale. Now under the Dutch flag again, *Astrid* is operated by the Traditional Sailing Charter Group of Harlingen as a charter and sail training vessel in Dutch and German waters.

SCANTLINGS
Length overall: 137' 6"
Beam: 22'
Draft: 8' 3"
Hull: Iron
Rig: Brig
Year built: 1918
Home port: Harlingen
Flag: Netherlands

SCANTLINGS
Length overall: 61'
Beam: 17' 6"
Draft: 9' 6"
Hull: Wood
Rig: Ketch
Year built: 1937
Home port: Öckerö
Flag: Sweden

ASTRID FINNE

Built in 1937 to join the famed fleet of the Norwegian ship rescue service, Norska Sjöröddningssällskapet, *Astrid Finne* carried sail number RS-43. She served in northern Norwegian waters until 1954, when she was acquired by the Swedish government to serve as a rescue and auxiliary service ship in the waters off Gotland.

In 1987, *Astrid Finne* was acquired by the school sailing association Mot Bättre Vetande, which means "toward better knowledge." She sails with her companion school ship, *Hawila,* providing youth fourteen to eighteen years of age a formal secondary school education together with a sail training program.

ATLANTICA

One of two ketches run by the Swedish group SKS Seglarskola, *Atlantica* was built in 1981 to be a sister ship to the agency's other vessel, *Gratitude*. She carries twenty-four youngsters on sail training cruises in the Baltic and North Seas.

SCANTLINGS
Length overall: 117'
Beam: 21' 6"
Draft: 11' 6"
Hull: Wood
Rig: Ketch
Year built: 1981
Home port: Göteborg
Flag: Sweden

ATLANTIS

Built in 1905 as the *Bürgermeister Bartels,* she ultimately served for eighty years as the *Elbe II* lightship, stationed at the mouth of the Elbe River. *Atlantis* was converted to her present rig in 1984–1985. As with other lightship conversions (see also *Alexander von Humboldt* and *Europa*), beauty—and the choice of an ideal rig—was in the eye of the beholder. In this case, the beholder was Capt. Hartmuth Paschburg, who planned *Atlantis* to be a traditional barquentine. In 1986 her sail plan was reduced, and the fore-royal sail and the main gaff sail were removed; finally, the gaff-topsail and main gaff were removed leaving only her square sails and staysails.

The *Atlantis* is German-owned and usually operates as a charter vessel in the Baltic and North Seas, although she has visited warmer waters for charter work. She has accommodations for fifteen crew members and thirty-four passengers.

SCANTLINGS
Length overall: 186'
Beam: 24' 6"
Draft: 16' 6"
Hull: Steel
Rig: Barquentine
Year built: 1905
Home port: Lübeck, Germany
Flag: Malta

BALTIC BEAUTY

Built originally as a motor trawler, *Baltic Beauty* fished the Baltic Sea for more than half a century. She then caught the eye of Victor Gottlow, who acquired her in 1978. It was this new owner-captain's dream to convert his engined workhorse into an elegant two-masted schooner. *Baltic Beauty* finally underwent an extensive three-year conversion that began in 1987. She emerged as a passenger-carrying sailboat, the *Dominic Fredion*. With a rough-hewn figurehead, she was renamed *Baltic Beauty* in her most recent service.

SCANTLINGS
Length overall: 131'
Beam: 16'
Draft: 9' 6"
Hull: Steel
Rig: Gaff-rigged schooner
Year built: 1926; converted, 1980
Home port: Ronneby
Flag: Sweden

SCANTLINGS
Length overall: 126'
Beam: 23'
Draft: 8' 6"
Hull: Wood
Rig: Topsail schooner
Year built: 1944
Home port: Brest, France
Flag: France

BEL ESPOIR II

Originally named *Nette S,* this wooden, three-masted schooner was built in 1944 by the Danish designer-shipwright J. Ring-Andersen to serve the fishing industry between the Faeroe Islands, Greenland, and Shetland. Renamed *Paedermost* in 1946, she was used to transport cattle between Hamburg and Copenhagen.

In 1955 this sturdy vessel was purchased by the Outward Bound Trust and renamed *Prince Louis II.* Under the trust's auspices, she served as home to the Moray Sea School in Scotland. In 1968 she was sold to a rehabilitation program in France known as Les Amis de Jeudi-Dimanche and renamed *Bel Espoir II.* The *Bel Espoir* has since become a haven for disadvantaged young people, providing them with an educational and sail training platform.

BELEM

Launched in 1896 for a South American freighter service, the *Belem* carried cocoa beans from Belem, Brazil, for a Paris chocolate maker. In 1913 she was purchased by the Duke of Westminster and converted to a yacht. A decade later, she was sold to Sir A. E. Guinness, renamed *Phantom II,* and rerigged as a staysail schooner. In 1979 she was acquired by the Association for the Preservation and Protection of Old French Ships, now the Belem Foundation, and restored as a barque.

SCANTLINGS
Length overall: 167'
Beam: 29'
Draft: 12' 6"
Hull: Steel
Rig: Barque
Year built: 1896
Home port: Nantes
Flag: France

LA BELLE POULE AND ÉTOILE

These sister schooners serve the French navy in the training of future officers, just as the Swedish navy uses the twin schooners *Flaken* and *Gladen*. Designed with the hull shape and the rigging of fishing vessels from Breton, *La Belle Poule* and *Étoile* were built in 1932 in the fishing port of Fécamp in northern Normandy, France.

During World War II, both vessels relocated to Portsmouth, England, where they served the Free France Forces. They are permitted to fly the French ensign with the imposed Cross of Lorraine in recognition of their service during the war.

SCANTLINGS
Length overall: 124'
Beam: 24'
Draft: 12'
Hull: Wood
Rig: Topsail schooner
Year built: 1932
Home port: Brest
Flag: France

BILL OF RIGHTS

Built in South Bristol, Maine, *Bill of Rights* spent her first two decades in Atlantic waters, first as a private charter vessel and then as a school training vessel. At the end of the 1990s, she weighed anchor for a new home port in Pacific waters.

Continuing her educational mission, *Bill of Rights* is operated now by the Los Angeles Maritime Institute, an affiliate of the Los Angeles Maritime Museum, and offers (along with sister ship *Pacific Swift*) programs for at-risk youth, as well as for groups of young people and adults. The schooner sails with crews of mariner educators who encourage the development of responsibility, self-discipline, persistence, patience, endurance, courage, and caution.

Designed on the lines of a classic schooner, the *Bill of Rights'* masts are set at a distinct rake, which defines her graceful profile.

SCANTLINGS
Length overall: 136'
Beam: 23'
Draft: 10'
Hull: Wood
Rig: Schooner
Year built: 1971
Home port: Los Angeles, California
Flag: United States

BLACK JACK

In 1954 Capt. Thomas G. Fuller of Ottawa purchased the steam tugboat *G. B. Patee II* from the Upper Ottawa Improvement Company. The tug, which was built in Scotland in 1904, had served for fifty years hauling logs. After an extensive refit, the vessel was transformed into a brigantine, renamed *Black Jack,* and operated as a private vessel.

In 1984, the new brigantine *Fair Jean* joined *Black Jack* to form the "fleet" of sail training vessels operated by Bytown Brigantine, Inc., of Ontario, Canada. The program offers sail training programs to youth in the Great Lakes area and the Caribbean.

SCANTLINGS
Length overall: 87'
Beam: 14'
Draft: 6'
Hull: Steel
Rig: Brigantine
Year built: 1904; converted, 1954
Home port: Ottawa, Ontario
Flag: Canada

BLACK PEARL

Completed in 1950 using surplus wood originally intended for the construction of World War II submarine chasers, *Black Pearl* crossed the picturesque entrance to Wickford Harbor on Narragansett Bay, Rhode Island, for years. Her clean, miniature lines added a new gloss to Coleridge's phrase from the *Rime of the Ancient Mariner* about a "painted ship upon a painted ocean" as she sat at anchor off Wickford.

In the late 1950s she was purchased by Barclay H. Warburton III, who sailed her to Kiel, Germany, in 1972 as the American representative to the tall ship events in Europe that summer. In 1973, Barclay founded the American Sail Training Association (ASTA), for which *Black Pearl* served as flagship.

Only 79 feet in sparred length, she is classified as an A-II vessel and is the smallest tall ship having square sails. *Black Pearl* is now operated by the Aquaculture Foundation of Bridgeport, Connecticut, as a sail training vessel.

SCANTLINGS
Length overall: 79'
Beam: 15'
Draft: 9'
Hull: Wood
Rig: Brigantine
Year built: 1951
Home port: Bridgeport,
   Connecticut
Flag: United States

BLUENOSE II

The original *Bluenose* was built in 1921 in the style of other Nova Scotia Grand Banks fishing schooners, but there was something special about her. She really did sail like the wind and proved it by winning the International Fishermen's Races cup for Canada several times. As a result, her likeness became a national symbol depicted on stamps and coins.

Designed by William Roué of Halifax, *Bluenose* was built at the Smith and Rhuland yard in Lunenburg. She worked and raced in North Atlantic waters until 1942, when she was sold for service as a freighter in the West Indies. She foundered on a reef off Haiti in 1946.

Bluenose II was built from the original plans of her predecessor and at the same yard in 1963. She serves as a sail training ship, as well as a goodwill ambassador for the Province of Nova Scotia. The schooner is operated by the *Bluenose II* Preservation Trust, a volunteer organization established to preserve *Bluenose II* and to maintain her legacy of traditional seamanship and ship building for future Nova Scotians.

In 1995, *Bluenose II* was restored by the Trust and pursues an active sailing schedule in north Atlantic waters. She berths at the Fisheries Museum of the Atlantic in Lunenburg, only a few blocks from the yard where she and the original *Bluenose* were built.

SCANTLINGS
Length overall: 161'
Beam: 27'
Draft: 16'
Hull: Wood
Rigging: Schooner
Year built: 1963
Home port: Lunenburg, Nova Scotia
Flag: Canada

BOA ESPERANZA

A replica of the fifteenth-century caravels that carried the Portuguese flag throughout the Mediterranean Sea, the south Atlantic, and the Indian Ocean, *Boa Esperanza*—"good hope"—was built and is maintained by APORVELA, the sail training association of Portugal. The most familiar caravel in the world is probably *Niña,* one of three ships that sailed in 1492 on Christopher Columbus's fateful journey of exploration. *Niña* was the smallest of the three ships and remained a *caravela latina* until square sails were added for stability on the ocean crossing and she became a *caravela rotunda*. Caravels originated in the Mediterranean and served largely as trading vessels from the fourteenth to the seventeenth centuries. Caravels have simple curved stems and plain transoms and are frequently lateen-rigged with long, tapering triangular sails. (Aficionados should note that there is not necessarily a relationship between the flush planked hulls we now refer to as *carvel*-built and the hulls of five centuries ago.) Caravels were used for the great explorations of Bartholomew Diaz in 1488 and Ferdinand Magellan's circumnavigation of 1519–1522.

SCANTLINGS
Length overall: 78'
Beam: 21' 6"
Draft: 10' 6"
Hull: Wood
Rig: Lateen
Year built: 1990
Home port: Lisbon
Flag: Portugal

SCANTLINGS
Length overall: 169'
Beam: 30'
Draft: 13'
Hull: Wood
Year built: 1960
Home port: Greenport, New York
Flag: United States

HMS BOUNTY

HMS *Bounty* was built in Lunenburg, Nova Scotia, in 1960 from the same Admiralty plans as for the original *Bounty* of 1788. The original merchant ship, captained by Lt. William Bligh, set out on a ten-month journey to collect breadfruit from Tahiti and transport it to the West Indies so that the owners of British plantations could inexpensively feed their workers. After leaving Tahiti, Acting Lt. Fletcher Christian and several crew members led a mutiny and took control of the boat. Bligh and his supporters safely returned to Britain in the boat's launch while the mutineers burned the ship and eventually settled on Pitcairn Island.

A replica of HMS *Bounty* was constructed for the 1962 MGM movie *Mutiny on the Bounty,* starring Marlon Brando and Trevor Howard. After serving as part of the MGM exhibit in St. Petersburg, Florida, she was acquired, along with the movie rights, by Ted Turner and the Turner Broadcasting System.

The fully rigged ship was donated to the Fall River (Massachusetts) Chamber Foundation in the early 1990s and after several years of financial uncertainty, *Bounty* was purchased by Robert Hansen, a Long Island, New York, businessman. Hansen plans to restore the *Bounty* to her former glory and create a sail training program on board.

Though she visually resembles her ill-fated namesake, this *Bounty* has auxiliary power in the form of two Caterpillar diesels and modern technological navigational systems and safety features to pass the rigorous standards of the United States Coast Guard. Arrangements are in progress to establish a home port in Greenport, New York.

BOWDOIN

A veteran of several scientific cruises into Arctic waters, this trim schooner was constructed with a specially reinforced hull to withstand the freezing grip of the icepack. After floundering between owners and restoration projects, *Bowdoin* has now found a more permanent home in Castine, Maine, with the Maine Maritime Academy. This sturdy, snub-nosed vessel serves as a classroom for high school students and educators studying marine and nautical sciences.

SCANTLINGS

Length overall: 101'
Beam: 21'
Draft: 10'
Hull: Wood
Rig: Schooner
Year built: 1921
Home port: Castine, Maine
Flag: United States

BRYZA H

Originally built as a rescue vessel in 1952, *Bryza H* was rebuilt and rerigged as a schooner in 2000 by her new owner, Waldemar Heisler. This wooden-hulled schooner is a welcome addition to the Baltic fleet. She carries up to twelve crew members in three cabins.

SCANTLINGS
Length overall: 75'
Beam: 17' 8"
Draft: 10' 6"
Hull: Wood
Rig: Schooner
Year built: 1952
Home port: Gdansk,
 Poland
Flag: Poland

SCANTLINGS
Length overall: 145'
Beam: 24' 6"
Draft: 9' 6"
Hull: Wood
Rig: Topsail schooner
Year built: 1984
Home port: Dana Point, California
Flag: United States

CALIFORNIAN

Californian is a full-scale re-creation of the nineteenth-century Revenue Marine Service cutter *C. W. Lawrence,* which was the first cutter assigned to the California coast. *Californian* was built by the Nautical Heritage Society at Spanish Landing, San Diego. Launched in May 1984, the vessel was christened and dedicated by Gloria Deukmejian, the wife of then-governor George Deukmejian. *Californian* exemplifies the speed and elegance of the Revenue Marine Service cutters of the past and the safety and service of present-day sail training school ships.

Designated by the California legislature as the official tall ship ambassador for the state of California, this topsail schooner has been active at special events throughout the state. Starting in the spring in northern California, she generally returns to southern waters by the end of summer.

The primary purpose of *Californian* is to serve as a special sail training vessel for fourth- through eighth-grade students, senior high school students, and college and university students of the entire state. While teaching the art and skill of sailing tall ships, *Californian* also provides an environment for students to experience self-reliance and teamwork.

LA CANCALAISE AND LA GRANVILLAISE

La Cancalaise and *La Granvillaise* are modern reproductions of traditional bisquines and were built by civic organizations in eponymous fishing villages on opposite sides of the Bay of St. Michel in Normandy, France. During the nineteenth century, hundreds of bisquines with shallow drafts and "gentle sails" fished the coves and crevices of the rugged Normandy coast. Bisquines are two-masted vessels with a foremast in "the eyes" and a retractable bowsprit. They are rigged with quadrilateral, loose-footed lugsails typical of Normandy. The head of the sail is narrower than the foot, and the luff is shorter than the leech.

The towns of Cancale and Granville commissioned two vessels in friendly competition to preserve the fishing and sailing heritage of their region. *La Cancalaise* was built in 1988, and *La Granvillaise* followed in 1990. These twin vessels present distinctive profiles in the tall ship fleet.

SCANTLINGS
Length overall: 55'
Beam: 15'
Draft: 8'
Hull: Wood
Rig: Bisquine
Years built: 1988 and 1990, respectively
Home port: Granville
Flag: France

CAPITAN MIRANDA

When launched in 1930 in Spain, *Capitan Miranda* began her career as a cargo vessel. She then served as a hydrographic survey ship for Uruguay's navy until 1978. Since that year the vessel has undergone a major refit and rededication as a school ship. With staysail schooner rigging and a clipper bow, *Capitan Miranda* was designed for speed and looks more like a private yacht than a traditional sail training ship.

The ship is named for the renowned hydrographer and educator Capt. Francisco P. Miranda (1868–1925), who served Uruguay as an officer, cabinet official, and war and navy secretary. He finished his distinguished career as professor of marine geography at the Naval Academy of Uruguay.

SCANTLINGS
Length overall: 205'
Beam: 27'
Draft: 12'
Hull: Steel
Rig: Staysail schooner
Year built: 1930
Home port: Montevideo
Flag: Uruguay

CAROLA

Built in 1900, *Carola* is an example of the hardy wooden vessel known in northern European waters as a galleass. These gaff-rigged ketches were typical trading vessels used to transport dry cargo between ports on the Baltic Sea, hence the classification Baltic trader. *Carola*'s hull was modified to carry wet cargo in 1926; as a *well smack,* water flowed through her hull. She was restored to her original design in 1969 and is now maintained by her proud owner, Capt. Hans Edwin Reith.

Carola participates frequently in tall ship gatherings on both sides of the Atlantic.

SCANTLINGS
Length overall: 82' 2"
Beam: 16'
Draft: 6'
Hull: Wood
Rig: Gaff ketch
Year built: 1900
Home port: Travemünde
Flag: Germany

CHRISTIAN RADICH

Christian Radich was a successful businessman and shipowner of Danish descent who died childless in 1889. He stipulated in his will that 50,000 kroner should be donated for the purpose of building a sail training ship for the youth of Norway. The funds were to be released only after the death of his wife, who lived on for twenty-seven years. By that time, the initial endowment had grown to 106,000 kroner, an amount large enough to provide much of the capital of the entire building fund. When the ship was finally christened in 1937, it was appropriate that it bear the name of its prescient donor, Christian Radich.

The *Christian Radich* is owned and administered by Østlandets Skoleskib, the East Coast Training Ship, although Norway's Ministry of Education is responsible for its operating expenses. For the past decade sail training has been integrated into the official Norwegian school system. Its basic curriculum is a full ten months of education for fifty cadets ranging in ages from eighteen to twenty-four; in addition, eighteen cooks become part of the training class. Generally, the coed ratio on board is forty-six males to forty-two females.

SCANTLINGS
Length overall: 205'
Beam: 36'
Draft: 15'
Hull: Steel
Rig: Ship
Year built: 1937
Home port: Oslo
Flag: Norway

SCANTLINGS
Length overall: 256'
Beam: 35'
Draft: 16'
Hull: Steel
Rig: Ship
Year built: 1999
Home port: Rio de Janeiro
Flag: Brazil

CISNE BRANCO

Cisne Branco, or "white swan," is the second of two "extreme clippers" built in the Damen shipyards of Amsterdam in 1999. (See also *Stad Amsterdam*.) Both have sharply raked bows, an overhanging stern to reduce hull contact with water, and carry a larger area of sail than is found in ships of comparable size.

Cisne Branco was built for the Brazilian navy and will train future officers. *Cisne Branco* takes its name from the lyrics of the Brazilian navy anthem that compares a navy vessel to the grace of a white swan. As a training vessel, *Cisne Branco* will accommodate 8 officers, 12 professional seamen, and 58 midshipmen.

Cisne Branco will make her maiden voyage in 2000 from Lisbon, Portugal, to Rio de Janeiro to commemorate the 500th anniversary of mercantile and maritime trade between Portugal and Brazil.

CLEARWATER

This replica recalls an era when ships powered by sails provided the primary mode of transportation on the Hudson River, which joins the Atlantic Ocean at New York City. Hudson River sloops, originally based on old Dutch designs, were single-masted, shallow-draught, centerboard boats that carried passengers and cargo. Until early in the nineteenth century they carried square topsails, but ultimately triangular topsails proved more manageable. Because river sailing often requires frequent tacking, or gybing, a sloop may change tacks more easily than other rigged vessels. A gybe—used when changing course while sailing before the wind—causes the boom to swing from one side of the vessel to the other. If executed carelessly a gybe can result in torn sails, damage to rigging, injury to crew, and in extreme cases, a dismasting.

Clearwater is owned and operated by Hudson River Sloop *Clearwater,* Inc., a nonprofit membership dedicated to defending and restoring the Hudson River and related waterways. The organization sponsors educational programs that focus on environmental and ecological issues. *Clearwater's* distinctive figurehead is a graceful Canada goose.

SCANTLINGS
Length overall: 106'
Beam: 25'
Draft: 8'
Hull: Wood
Rig: Sloop
Year built: 1969
Home port: Poughkeepsie, New York
Flag: United States

CLIPPER CITY

Clipper City is a replica of a nineteenth-century coasting schooner that carried coal and lumber between American ports on the east coast. Adapted for the twentieth century, this 158-foot topsail schooner has a steel hull instead of the wooden one of her namesake and predecessor.

With her clipper bow and square topsails, *Clipper City* recalls the famed clipper ships that made Baltimore a sailing and mercantile center of the nineteenth century, sending ships to and from the Californian gold fields and expanding trade in the West Indies and South America.

Clipper City is owned by a private chartering agency and provides daily tours of the historic harbor and upper Chesapeake Bay. She also participates in major maritime festivals along the east coast of the United States.

SCANTLINGS
Length overall: 158'
Beam: 27'
Draft: 6' 6"
Hull: Steel
Rig: Topsail schooner
Year built: 1985
Home port: Baltimore, Maryland
Flag: United States

CONCORDIA

A steel-hulled barquentine, *Concordia* was built to serve as the flagship of Canada's Class Afloat Foundation. Operating from regional headquarters on both the Atlantic and Pacific coasts, *Concordia* offers a full-time scholastic program as part of extended voyages between the North and South Pacific and the Atlantic and the Caribbean Oceans. On her maiden voyage in 1992 she participated in the Grand Columbus Regatta. After voyages to the South Pacific from her base in Vancouver, British Columbia, *Concordia* has returned to Atlantic waters and her eastern home at West Island College in Pointe Claire, Quebec.

SCANTLINGS
Length overall: 185'
Beam: 30'
Draft: 13' 2"
Hull: Steel
Rig: Barquentine
Year built: 1992
Home port: Quebec
Flag: Canada

SCANTLINGS
Length overall: 204'
Beam: 43' 6"
Draft: 22' 5"
Hull: Wood
Rig: Ship
Year built: 1797
Home port: Boston,
  Massachusetts
Flag: United States

USS CONSTITUTION

The most famous and most enduring tall ship in America, the USS *Constitution* was one of six warships commissioned by President George Washington to protect the young nation's maritime interests and shores. Authorized by Congress in 1794, she was built at Edmund Hartt's shipyard near Boston's Old North Church. The copper for many of her fittings came from a mill operated by patriot Paul Revere.

The ship was so large that some sailors doubted she would be of practical value, but she proved herself both strong and fast (with a top speed of 13.5 knots). Her original specifications put her at 204 feet long overall (175 feet on the waterline) and gave her thirty-six sails with an area of 42,270 square feet, forty-four guns (although she often carried fifty) with a range of 1,200 yards, and a crew of 450. She was completed in 1797 at a cost—including her figurehead, which represents Hercules with a raised club—of $320,718.84.

Thwarting Barbary pirates in the Mediterranean and repelling French privateers in the Caribbean, *Constitution* proved to be an eminently serviceable vessel. She earned her legendary nickname, Old Ironsides, in the War of 1812 when British frigates were frustrated to see their cannonballs bounce off her 21-inch oak-planked hull.

After serving as the flagship of the American fleet in the Mediterranean, *Constitution* was removed from active service in 1828. Two years later, the U.S. Navy judged her unseaworthy. She was saved only by congressional intervention after an outcry of public support, spurred by publication of the poem "Old Ironsides," by Oliver Wendell Holmes. She was rebuilt in 1855, restored in 1871, and served as a Navy training ship for several years before her active career came to an end. Largely forgotten, she sat decomposing at a pier in the Portsmouth, New Hampshire, Naval Shipyard. There was a proposal to tow her to sea as a target for gunnery practice. After appropriating limited money for repairs in 1906, Congress finally agreed to supplement the money raised by school children from around the United States to pay for a complete rebuilding of *Constitution* between 1927 and 1930. Then, on 2 July 1931, towed by a mine sweeper, *Constitution* began a national tour that took her from Maine to Washington through the Panama Canal. She called on ninety ports and received some 4.5 million visitors. Three years later, she took up a permanent station at the now-retired Boston Naval Shipyard in Charlestown, Massachusetts, where she remains the nation's oldest ship in active commission and a national historic landmark.

Old Ironsides "sails" Boston harbor annually for her maintenance turnaround; she is turned so that her port and starboard sides weather evenly at dockside. During the past decade this event has been scheduled to coincide with gatherings of the international tall ship fleet in Boston Harbor. *Constitution* underwent her most recent major refitting and restoration in preparation for marking the celebration of her bicentennial year in 1997.

CORONET

One of the great private yachts of the gilded age of the turn of the century, *Coronet* circumnavigated the globe twice, raced for international cups, and served as a missionary vessel for a Christian fellowship.

Built to rigorous standards in 1885, *Coronet*'s design called for a "plumb stem," structural strength, and speed. Keel, keelson, frames, and planks were all of white oak from Maine. In addition to the pine of her cabin ceilings, the finest teak was used for her stanchions, and mahogany of exceptional density and grain from Honduras was fashioned for the brightwork of her rails and deckhouses. At the height of her sailing career in the 1890s she was owned by Newport philanthropist Arthur Curtis James and went on to serve as flagship for the New York Yacht Club.

After a hundred years of sailing she was recently acquired by the International Yacht Restoration School, which was founded by Elizabeth Meyers. Returned to Newport, Rhode Island, an extensive restoration program has begun to return *Coronet* to her former glory.

SCANTLINGS
Length overall: 133'
Beam: 27'
Draft: 12' 6"
Hull: Wood
Rig: Schooner
Year built: 1885
Home port: Newport, Rhode Island
Flag: United States

CORWITH CRAMER

Corwith Cramer is a 134-foot steel-hulled brigantine designed specifically to meet the requirements of accredited programs for high school and college-level students run by the Sea Education Association in Woods Hole, Massachusetts. *Corwith Cramer* is one of two vessels that fulfills the at-sea portion of SEA's programs in oceanography and marine science.

The other vessel, *Westward,* was built as a private yacht. Her design and sheer were incorporated into the more functional design of *Corwith Cramer,* which was built in 1987 in Bilbao, Spain, to the design specifications of Woodin & Marean of Wiscosset, Maine.

SCANTLINGS
Length overall: 134'
Beam: 26'
Draft: 13'
Hull: Steel
Rig: Brigantine
Year built: 1987
Home port: Woods Hole,
   Massachusetts
Flag: United States

CREOLE

One of the most beautiful and biggest private yachts ever made, *Creole* has had a varied career that has seen her ownership shift between some of the wealthiest sailing families in the world and fledgling educational programs for disadvantaged youth. From the Greek shipping magnate Stavros Niarchos, her fortunes brought her to the Nyborg Sail Training School in Denmark. In the past decade millions of dollars have been spent to refurbish her to her former elegance by the Gucci family of Italy, but her present situation remains uncertain.

SCANTLINGS
Length overall: 215'
Beam: 31'
Draft: 19'
Hull: Steel
Rig: Staysail schooner
Year built: 1927
Home port: Uncertain
Flag: Italy

SCANTLINGS
Length overall: 221'
Beam: 32' 6"
Draft: 15' 6"
Hull: Steel
Rig: Schooner
Year built: 1937
Home port: Lisbon
Flag: Portugal

CREOULA

Creoula is a four-masted, steel-hulled schooner built in 1937 in a record sixty-two workdays. She was constructed for a Portuguese fishing company, Parceria Geral de Pescarias, and until her last trip in 1973, *Creoula* had wooden topmasts, booms, and gaffs. The standing rigging has always been steel, and the running rigging was originally made from sisal rope.

Until 1973, this four-masted schooner spent thirty-seven consecutive years working the cold waters off Grand Banks, Newfoundland. The ship typically set sail from Lisbon in April for Nova Scotia, where she remained until the end of May. After renewing supplies in Sidney, Nova Scotia, or St. John's, Newfoundland, *Creoula* would sail to Greenland, where she fished until mid-September, often reaching a latitude of 48° off the western coast of Greenland. If her holds were not full, she fished again off Newfoundland until mid-October and then returned to Portugal with 800 tons of salted fish and 60 tons of cod-liver oil. At the fishing grounds she launched one-person dories. Often the fishers took dogs with them; their barking helped *Creoula* to find them in the fog.

In 1979 she was purchased from the Portuguese Department of Fisheries with the intention of converting her to a museum of fishery. A survey showed her hull to be in impeccable condition, however, and a decision was made to restore her as a sail training vessel. She is now owned by the Portuguese navy but carries only civilian cadets and trainees.

In 1992, *Creoula* was modified slightly, and a portion of the original crew's quarters amidship was converted to a classroom and library.

CUAUHTEMOC

Named for the last of the Aztec emperors, this new barque represents the Mexican navy. *Cuauhtemoc* is one of four barques built for Latin American nations to serve as goodwill ambassadors and training schools for their respective navies. The other members of the quartet are *Gloria* of Columbia (1968), *Guayas* of Ecuador (1977), and *Simon Bolivar* of Venezuela (1980). Last of the four, built in 1982, *Cuauhtemoc* was constructed in the famed shipyard Astilleros y Talleres Celaya, S.A., Bilbao, Spain.

SCANTLINGS
Length overall: 270'
Draft: 17' 1"
Beam: 39' 4"
Rig: Barque
Hull: Steel
Year built: 1982
Home port: Acapulco
Flag: Mexico

DANMARK

Danmark is a familiar visitor to the United States. This 249-foot ship serves the Danish Marine Authority from her home port in Copenhagen.

On a visit to New York in 1939, *Danmark*'s captain, Knud Hansen, offered the services of the ship to the United States. Hansen wanted to avoid surrendering her to Axis powers and to ensure her safety during the war years. During World War II, *Danmark* served as a school ship at the U.S. Coast Guard Academy in New London, Connecticut, training future Coast Guard and Navy officers. After the war, she was sailed back to Denmark, but a few Danes returned to the United States and made their homes in the New London area. Several of them assisted the Coast Guard in sailing a similar vessel, a barque, USCGC *Eagle*, formerly *Horstwessel*, from Bremerhaven, Germany, to the United States.

A model of the *Danmark*, symbolizing her service to the United States, graced the Oval Office during the presidency of John F. Kennedy.

SCANTLINGS
Length overall: 253'
Beam: 33'
Draft: 15'
Hull: Steel
Rig: Ship
Year built: 1933
Home port: Copenhagen
Flag: Denmark

DAR MLODZIEZY

Dar Mlodziezy ("gift of youth") is a full-rigged, 360-foot ship designed by the distinguished Polish naval architect Zygmunt Choren and is the flagship of the Merchant Marine Academy (Wyzsza Szkola Morska) in Gdynia, Poland. *Dar Mlodziezy* was funded in part by the contributions of elementary school children during the 1960s and 1970s. Commissioned in 1982, she replaced the venerable *Dar Pomorza* ("gift of Pomorze," a reference to the coastal region of Poland), which served Poland for more than six decades before her retirement. *Dar Pomorza* participated in Operation Sail in 1976.

Dar Mlodziezy's distinctive design served as the prototype for a class of vessels (five in all) built in Gdansk for the Russian confederation of the 1980s. Four of the five vessels—*Mir, Druzhba, Pallada,* and *Nasheba*—now fly the Russian flag, while *Khersones* flies the flag of Ukraine. These are true sister ships and vary only slightly in dimensions and configuration.

SCANTLINGS
Length overall: 360'
Beam: 45' 9"
Draft: 20' 7"
Hull: Steel
Rig: Ship
Year built: 1982
Home port: Gdynia
Flag: Poland

SCANTLINGS
Length overall: 148'
Beam: 21' 4"
Draft: 11' 6"
Hull: Wood
Rig: Schooner
Year built: 1902
Home port: Vamdrup
Flag: Denmark

DEN STORE BJØRN

Den Store Bjørn takes her name from the constellation Ursa Major. Originally built as a lightship in 1902, *Den Store Bjørn* was towed to a fixed position and therefore did not have an engine, although she was refitted with one in 1959. Finally taken out of navigational service, she was bought in 1980 by the Danish Schooner Cooperative. She is now operated by Smaskolen Fremtidens Danmark/Sofolkene (Small School for Future Danish Seafolk), and she carries five permanent officers and crew members, three teachers, and twelve trainees, ranging in ages from sixteen to twenty.

In addition to practical courses in seamanship and the marine sciences, students receive instruction in the compulsory curriculum of the Danish elementary school system.

SCANTLINGS
Length overall: 134'
Beam: 23' 6"
Draft: 8' 9"
Hull: Wood
Rig: Three-masted schooner
Year built: 2000
Home port: Milwaukee, Wisconsin
Flag: United States

DENIS SULLIVAN

Named for a famed Great Lakes schooner captain of the early twentieth century, *Denis Sullivan* was designed and built under the auspices of the Wisconsin Lake Schooner Education Association (WLSEA) of Milwaukee, Wisconsin. The graceful lines of this three-masted schooner are based on those of traditional nineteenth-century lake schooners that carried a variety of cargo on the Great Lakes as recently as World War I.

Denis Sullivan provides educational and sail-training programs for students of all ages. Touted as "Wisconsin's Flagship," she represents Milwaukee and the state of Wisconsin as a goodwill ambassador to the world.

DEWA RUCI

Originally ordered from a German yard in 1932, *Dewa Ruci*'s construction was delayed by the advent of World War II until the yard itself, heavily damaged, could be repaired. Finally completed two decades after the original order was placed, *Dewa Ruci* serves as a sail training vessel for the Indonesian navy. Her figurehead and name represent the mythological Indonesian god of courage and sincerity. Sailing from her home port in the Indian Ocean, *Dewa Ruci* makes one of the longest journeys of any vessel to participate in American and European tall ship events.

SCANTLINGS
Length overall: 191'
Beam: 31'
Draft: 13'
Hull: Steel
Rig: Barquentine
Year built: 1952
Home port: Jakarta
Flag: Indonesia

SCANTLINGS
Length overall: 108' 5"
Beam: 21'
Draft: 9' 6"
Hull: Wood
Rig: Ketch
Year built: 1889
Home port: Tenerife,
   Canary Islands
Flag: Norway

DRYAFJELD

One of the oldest vessels in the international fleet, *Dryafjeld* (formerly the *Anna Kristina*) was built near Kristiansand, Norway, in 1889.
Local pine forests were the source of some six hundred trees that provided wood for her keel and planking.

Dryafjeld, which is the ship's original name, is known as a *hardanger jakt,* after the fjord area in Norway where such vessels were first built. Because they were usually built and owned by farmers who had substantial supplies of timber, these vessels were solidly constructed. *Dryafjeld* has a double hull of Norwegian pine and a full frame, with timbers spaced 1 to 4 inches apart. Hardanger jakts were rigged as sloops or ketches. *Dryafjeld* is rigged as a ketch, with her mizzenmast between the galley and the captain's cabin. She carries a square topsail.

Her sails were traditionally made from cotton or flax and tanned to preserve them against the mildew and rot to which natural fibers are susceptible, hence their yellow-brown color. The twentieth century has prevailed, however, and *Dryafjeld*'s sails are now made from a synthetic fiber, Duradon, which makes them lighter and more manageable than those of cotton or flax. Their traditional coloring, however, has been retained.

SCANTLINGS
Length overall: 72'
Beam: 11'
Draft: 6' 5"
Hull: Wood
Rig: Gaff-rigged yawl
Year built: 1912
Home port: Ipswich,
    England
Flag: United Kingdom

DUET

Christened *Gaviota,* this classic Edwardian yacht was built in 1912 at White's Yard on the River Itchen in Southampton, England. She retains many of her original features, including teak decks and her rig. The gaff-rigged yawl was purchased in the early 1930s by the explorer Augustine Courtland and renamed *Duet.* Upon Courtland's death in 1959, *Duet* was passed to his son, the Reverend Christopher Courtauld, who co-founded the Ocean Youth Club in 1960. *Duet* served as part of the Youth Club's adventure sail training fleet for nearly 35 years until being loaned to the Cirdan Sailing Trust in 1994 for sail training.

With a professional crew of two plus seven trainees, *Duet* is one of the smallest in the tall ship fleet but holds her own against larger vessels. Her youthful crew represents the Cirdan Sailing Trust with spark and energy.

SCANTLINGS
Length overall: 295'
Beam: 39'
Draft: 17'
Hull: Steel
Rig: Barque
Year built: 1936
Home port: New London,
   Connecticut
Flag: United States

EAGLE

Flagship of the U.S. Coast Guard Academy, *Eagle* also serves as an international goodwill ambassador for the United States. *Eagle*'s primary mission is training U.S. Coast Guard cadets in the fundamental disciplines of seamanship. Through practical application, cadets learn navigation, engineering, and ship maneuvering. In addition, they set some 20,000 square feet of sail and control more than 20 miles of rigging lines while under way.

The *Eagle* was originally named *Horst Wessel* and was one of four German sister training ships built in the famous Blohm & Voss shipyard in Hamburg during the 1930s. She came under the U.S. flag at the conclusion of World War II. Her sister ships, still part of the international fleet, are *Sagres II* (Portugal), *Mircea* (Romania), *Tovarishch* (Ukraine), and *Gorch Fock II* (Germany), built in 1958 from the same plans and design as the *Eagle*.

Today, *Eagle*'s home port is New London, Connecticut, but she is just as likely to be seen in ports and harbors around the world representing the United States at tall ship gatherings and other international events.

SCANTLINGS
Length overall: 194'
Beam: 40'
Draft: 16'
Hull: Steel
Rig: Schooner
Year built: 1989
Home port: Scheveningen
Flag: Netherlands

EENDRACHT II

Eendracht II is the second vessel operated by Het Zeilend Zeeschip, a national society and a nonprofit foundation that promotes the maritime traditions of the Netherlands. The organization's sail training programs for people ages fifteen to twenty-five years began in 1974 with the original *Eendracht*, a two-masted schooner whose name means unity and teamwork in Dutch. By 1986, the demand for training activities had outgrown the vessel. She was sold to a German group, rechristened *Johann Smidt*, and Het Zeilend commissioned a new three-masted schooner. After several years of planning, the keel of *Eendracht II* was laid in 1988. A year later, the new vessel was commissioned and blessed by Her Majesty Queen Beatrix.

Built of steel to a Dutch design, the schooner was planned for safe handling during sail training and is certified for unrestricted worldwide sailing. *Eendracht II* sails from May to November in north European waters, and from December to April in the Mediterranean. In addition to four paid crew members, *Eendracht II* carries up to fourteen volunteer staff and as many as forty trainees.

ELEANOR MARY

Built at Nova Scotia's famous Covey Island Boatworks, *Eleanor Mary* was based on the designs of the pilot cutters that sailed in the Bristol Channel during the early twentieth century, most notably *Marguerite, Hirta,* and *Kindly Light.*

Eleanor Mary made her maiden voyage in 1998. She can accommodate up to seven guests.

SCANTLINGS
Length overall: 70'
Beam: 14'
Draft: 8'
Hull: Wood and epoxy
Rig: Cutter
Year built: 1997
Home port: Cowes, England
Flag: United Kingdom

ELENA–MARIA–BARBARA

A replica of the nineteenth-century schooners that sailed the waters of the eastern Baltic Sea, *Elena–Maria–Barbara* is a tall ship with a Russian perspective. Considerably smaller than the barques and fully rigged ships in the Russian fleet, *Elena–Maria–Barbara* appears almost tiny by comparison, but she represents a hardy class of sailing vessel that operated out of St. Petersburg a century ago. Note her exaggerated jibboom, which extends more than 30 feet from her bow. This vessel was built and is supported by an avid sailing club in St. Petersburg.

SCANTLINGS
Length overall: 97'
Beam: 16'
Draft: 8'
Hull: Wood
Rig: Schooner
Year built: 1992
Home port: St. Petersburg
Flag: Russia

SCANTLINGS
Length overall: 202'
Beam: 28'
Draft: 16'
Hull: Iomore iron and welded steel
Rig: Barque
Year built: 1877
Home port: Galveston, Texas
Flag: United States

ELISSA

The pride of the Galveston Historical Foundation, *Elissa* is one of the few remaining iron-hulled vessels still sailing. She enjoyed a long career as a cargo vessel, which saw her registered under six different flags, beginning in Scotland in 1877 and ending as a demasted motor vessel in the Greek Islands. Her hull was found in the Mediterranean awaiting a scrapper's acetylene torch by the late archaeologist Peter Throckmorton, through whose efforts and advocacy she was purchased by the foundation in 1975. *Elissa* was brought to Texas in 1979 and now makes Galveston—a port she had visited under other flags more than a century ago—her home port.

SCANTLINGS
Length overall: 143' 5"
Beam: 29' 2"
Draft: 11' 2"
Hull: Wood
Rig: Ship
Year built: 1988–1993
Home port: Sydney, Australia
Flag: Australia

HM BARK ENDEAVOUR

Instances of ship reincarnation are rare, but *Endeavour* is a remarkable example. Captain James Cook sailed the original *Endeavour* from 1768 to 1771 on the first of his three voyages of Pacific exploration. Milestones of this adventure included overcoming scurvy, accurately calculating ship's longitude at sea for the first time, and charting the islands of New Zealand and the east coat of Australia. Two centuries later, a group of Australians decided to recreate *Endeavour*. Because very accurate 18th century records of the original ship existed, it was possible to build an exact replica. Constructed in Fremantle, Western Australia from Australian hardwoods and American Douglas fir, the *Endeavour*'s only concessions to the 20th century are modern heads, showers, electric galley, machinery, and freezers. The crew lives and works the ship just as they would have done two centuries ago.

ERNESTINA

Originally named *Effie M. Morrissey*, *Ernestina* began as a Grand Banks, Newfoundland, fishing schooner. After twenty-five years of service, she was acquired by Capt. Robert Bartlett, who used her for Arctic exploration in 1925. Over the next twenty years she served in northern waters and even held a commission in the United States Navy during World War II.

After the war, under the helm of Capt. Henrique Mendes, she made more than twelve passages from the Cape Verde Islands to the United States carrying cargo and immigrants. A sturdy wooden-hulled schooner, *Ernestina* sailed through many storms, but none compared with the treacherous difficulties she experienced in recent years trying to survive and sustain herself. At one point, precarious finances prompted a crew to abandon the vessel at dockside in Miami, Florida.

In 1982 she was donated by the Republic of Cape Verde to the people of the United States, her title to be held by the Commonwealth of Massachusetts. In recognition of her distinguished history and service, *Ernestina* is now an historic landmark. Berthed at New Bedford, Massachusetts, she is used to present historical, educational, and maritime programs.

SCANTLINGS

Length overall: 156'
Beam: 25'
Draft: 13'
Hull: Wood
Rig: Schooner
Year built: 1894
Home port: New Bedford, Massachusetts
Flag: United States

ESMERALDA

The pride of the Chilean navy, *Esmeralda* was built in Cadiz, Spain, from plans used to build Spain's *Juan Sebastian de Elcano*. Both vessels were constructed from a Camper & Nicholson design at the same yard, though some twenty-seven years apart–Echevarrieta y Larriñaga in Cadiz. The only differences between these two elegant four-masters are the additional fore-and-aft sail on the *Sebastian's* foremast, designating her as a topsail schooner, and the slightly flatter angle of *Esmeralda's* bowsprit.

Esmeralda was completed in 1954. Her distinctive figurehead represents a giant Andes condor, the national bird of Chile.

SCANTLINGS
Length overall: 371'
Beam: 42' 8"
Draft: 19' 8"
Hull: Steel
Rig: Four-masted barquentine
Year built: 1952–1954
Home port: Valparaiso
Flag: Chile

ÉTOILE MOLENE

Appearing to be a gaff ketch, this 115-foot wooden vessel is proudly called a Dundée thonier by her captain, Robert Escoffier, of St. Mâlo. She is distinguished from other European ketches by her retractable bowsprit. Built in 1954, she wears the traditional yellow sails of the Brest region of France. Her name means star of Molene and refers to a snug harbor near Brest, France.

SCANTLINGS
Length overall: 115'
Beam: 21' 4"
Draft: 12' 6"
Hull: Wood
Rig: Dundée thonier
Year built: 1954
Home port: St. Mâlo
Flag: France

EUROPA

This charming barque exudes Old World warmth and ambiance and is another of the many conversions to sail made in recent decades. Originally a lightship in the North Sea, *Europa* is now a commercial charter vessel sailing from Rotterdam. She is named for the Greek mythological figure Europa, who infatuated the god Jupiter with her beauty. He appeared to her as a lovable bull and carried her off to Crete. After bearing him two children, Jupiter named the continent of Europe in her honor. *Europa's* figurehead depicts the legendary beauty whose name she carries.

Built in 1911 in Hamburg, Germany, *Europa* was acquired in 1987 and rebuilt for her recent service as a private charter vessel. Operating out of the Netherlands, *Europa* makes worldwide sailing passages with fifty passengers.

In 2002, she changed ownership and departed on a lengthy cruise which will include visits to Korea; Japan; Richmond, British Columbia; Seattle, Washington; San Francisco; Los Angeles; and San Diego as part of the Tall Ships Challenge of 2002.

SCANTLINGS
Length overall: 180'
Beam: 24' 6"
Draft: 12' 6"
Hull: Steel
Rig: Barque
Year built: 1911
Home port: Rotterdam
Flag: Holland

EXCELSIOR

The Lowestoft "smack," or "dandy," is a sailing trawler with noteworthy characteristics. Its heavy construction and long, straight keel permit long stays at sea in all weather. Being deep-drafted and having a moderate ratio of beam to length make the design both "sea-kindly" and fast.

The ketch rig is unusual on smacks in that both masts are raked forward, allowing great versatility in the setting of sails. The sail plan can be varied to suit conditions, and the disposition of the sails balances the helm.

In 1971 *Excelsior* (LT 472) was serving as a motor coaster, carrying cargo around Norway. She was acquired by the *Excelsior* Trust with the intention of making her an active, seagoing sailing vessel. With the aid of many local firms and the sponsorship by the Manpower Services Commission in Lowestoft, a thorough renovation of her hull and upper works (including rigging) was completed in 1988.

Excelsior is tiller-steered on an open deck, though she now has bulwarks to provide safety and security at sea. Despite appearances, the traditional tan sails and running rigging are made from synthetic fibers, which are naturally colored. These lines last longer and are safer because they resist the dangers of rot and mildew associated with hemp and flax.

SCANTLINGS
Length overall: 108' 6"
Beam: 19' 3"
Draft: 8' 6"
Hull: Wood
Rig: Ketch
Year built: 1921
Home port: Lowestoft
Flag: United Kingdom

EYE OF THE WIND

This square-rigged, iron-hulled vessel was originally a topsail schooner, built for the South American hide trade in 1911. In 1923 she was sold to Swedish owners and for the next 50 years served as a Baltic trader in the Baltic and North Seas.

In 1973 *Eye of the Wind* was purchased by a private, five-member syndicate that restored and furnished her to serve as the flagship of Operation Drake in the South Pacific. Along with an appearance in the First Fleet Reenactment to celebrate Australia's centenary, this brigantine again rounded Cape Horn in December 1991 to take part in the Grand Columbus Regatta of 1992.

With her tanbark sails and colorful pennants flying from her mainmast, *Eye of the Wind* is an active and attractive addition to the international fleet of tall ships. Her figurehead is a "wind cherub," designed and carved by one of her original partners, Rodney Clarke, of Redfern, Australia. Along with the spirit of adventure of the crew, the cherub is a welcome addition to this striking brigantine-brig. She is often square-rigged on one or both of her masts. *Eye of the Wind* starred in the recent movie *White Squall*.

In 2001, *Eye of the Wind* changed owners and underwent an extensive refit in Denmark before resuming a sailing program out of Devon, England.

SCANTLINGS
Length overall: 132'
Beam: 23'
Draft: 9'
Hull: Iron
Rig: Brigantine
Year built: 1911
Home port: Faversham, Kent, England
Flag: United Kingdom

KRUZENSHTERN

PEKING

PASSAT

THE "FLYING P" LINE

Fast, commodious clipper ships were still being built for commercial trade well into the first years of the twentieth century. The F. Laeisz Company of Hamburg, Germany, is notable for assembling one of the great fleets of these remarkable vessels. Founded in 1836 by Reederei Ferdinand Laeisz, the line came to be known as the Flying P, after the owner's penchant for choosing names for his vessels that began with the letter *P*. The tradition started in 1862 when Laeisz christened a ship *Pudel*, after his daughter-in-law. During the next eighty years sixty-seven vessels, wood and steel, flew the Flying P pennant.

Of the line's exceptional vessels were the five-masted barque *Potosi* (1895) and the world's only five-masted, full-rigged ship, *Preussen* (1902). Beginning in 1903, the F. Laeisz Company commissioned a series of barques that came to be known as the Eight Sisters: *Pangani* (1903), *Petschili* and *Pamir* (1905), *Peking* and *Passat* (1911), *Pola* (1916), *Priwall* (1917), and *Padua* (1926).

These barques were among the last of the deepwater sailing vessels to navigate the great trade routes of the Atlantic and Pacific Oceans. They carried bulk cargoes of fuel and manufactured goods to South America and Australia and returned with nitrate that had been mined in Chile and grain from Australia.

Four of the Eight Sisters have survived, and one, *Padua*, renamed *Kruzenshtern* (see separate entry), is still actively sailing. The other Flying P's are maintained as museum ships in sites around the world: *Peking* (length overall: 377 feet) at the South Street Seaport Museum in New York; *Passat* (length overall: 377 feet) at the Travemunde Maritime Museum in Germany; and *Pommern* (length overall: 350 feet) at the Museifartyget Pommern in Mariehamn in Finland. The F. Laeisz Company still operates in Hamburg.

POMMERN

SCANTLINGS
Length overall: 46'
Beam: 10' 6"
Draft: 4' 6"
Hull: Ferro-cement
Rig: Junk schooner
Year built: 1978
Home port: Solomon's Island, Maryland
Flag: United States

FOON YIN

This singular junk-rigged schooner is made from ferro-cement. Her name means "welcome" in Chinese.
Combining unique materials with a unique rig, *Foon Yin* is an example of the infinite variations seen in both old
and new sailing vessels. Her Chinese red lugsails are a colorful addition to many seascapes.

SCANTLINGS
Length overall: 101'
Beam: 16' 10"
Draft: 8' 9"
Rig: Tops'l Sloop
Hull: Wood
Year built: 2004
Homeport: South Haven, Michigan
Flag: United States

FRIENDS GOOD WILL

The original sloop *Friends Good Will* was built as a Great Lakes trader. In 1812, she carried supplies to Fort Dearborn (now Chicago) from Mackinac Island, unaware that America had recently declared war on Great Britain. Returning to Mackinac, she was captured by the British navy.

English control of Lakes Michigan and Huron weakened America's claim to the Northwest Territory, so the U.S. Navy constructed a small Great Lakes fleet. Breaking a British blockage in July 1813, this fleet—led by Commodore Oliver Hazard Perry—bested the British. He wrote, "We have met the enemy and they are ours." *Little Belt* served the U.S. Navy until burned by the British.

The present *Friends Good Will* was built at the Scarano Brothers Boatyard in Albany for the Michigan Maritime Museum. The design combines modern construction with the features of a nineteenth-century sloop. To sail on the sloop, contact the museum (see p. 223).

FRYDERYK CHOPIN

This elegant brig is named for the nineteenth-century Polish composer and pianist. Designed by the naval architect Zygmunt Choren to the specifications of Capt. Krysztof Baranowski, *Fryderyk Chopin* combines maximum sail area and speed with stability and safety for educational programs. Measuring 182 feet long overall, with masts soaring 125 feet above her deck, *Fryderyk Chopin* is rigged to carry six jib sails along with its high skysails.

The filigree of her standing rigging and the number of sails she carries make *Fryderyk Chopin* ideal for sail training and require concentrated effort from her disciplined crews. On her maiden voyage and first Atlantic crossing in 1992, she participated in Operation Sail in New York and also visited Boston, Massachusetts, and Newport, Rhode Island.

SCANTLINGS

Length overall: 182'
Beam: 28'
Draft: 12' 6"
Hull: Steel
Rig: Brig
Year built: 1992
Home port: Szczecin
Flag: Poland

GAZELA PHILADELPHIA

Built in Portugal in 1883 as the *Gazela Primerio,* this 178-foot barquentine worked the Grand Banks fishing grounds off Newfoundland for nearly a century before her acquisition and restoration by the Ship Preservation Guild of Philadelphia. She is the oldest wooden square-rigger still in active service.

During her fishing career she carried a crew of forty men to the Grand Banks, where thirty-five one-person dories rowed out to net cod. Each day the fish caught were cleaned, salted, and stored until the ship's 350-ton capacity was reached and the six-month voyage completed.

The ship was originally constructed of two types of pine, "stone" pine and "marine" pine, which were cultivated for their qualities of close-grain and hardness in special forests planted by order of Prince Henry the Navigator in the fourteenth century.

In Philadelphia she hosts programs on ship preservation, sail training, and marine science for youngsters and volunteers. *Gazela Philadelphia* is the city's maritime ambassador to national and international events, and she also serves as a museum of sailing ship technology.

SCANTLINGS
Length overall: 178'
Beam: 27'
Draft: 17'
Hull: Wood
Rig: Barquentine
Year built: 1883
Home port: Philadelphia, Pennsylvania
Flag: United States

GEFION

Built as a Baltic trading vessel in Denmark in 1932, *Gefion* was converted from a *haj kutter* (a traditional fishing rig) in 1986 to a small cruising ketch for charter and sail training. Now registered in Kiel, Germany, *Gefion*'s red hull is a familiar part of major tall ship festivals on the Baltic and North Seas.

The name "Gefion" is from a myth of the islands bordering the shoreline of the Baltic Sea. When King Gylfi ruled the lands that are now called Sweden, he gave a plowland in his kingdom—whatever four oxen could plow in a day and a night—to a beggar-woman as a reward for the way she had entertained him. *Gefion*, a goddess disguised as the beggar woman, was rewarded with an opportunity to "map out her own farm" and, with the help of her four sons (their father was a giant) posing as oxen, created the trough that separates the island of Seeland (Zealand) from the Danish coast.

SCANTLINGS
Length overall: 69'
Beam: 14'
Draft: 8' 3"
Rig: Schooner
Hull: Wood
Year built: 1932
Home port: Kiel
Flag: Germany

GEORG STAGE

Two small fully rigged ships have carried the name *Georg Stage*. The first was built in 1882 and is now moored at Mystic Seaport in Connecticut. She was renamed the *Joseph Conrad* by the famed Australian sea captain Alan Villiers. The present *Georg Stage* is a fully rigged ship built between 1934 and 1935 at the Fredrikshavn shipyard in northern Denmark. Both ships were named in honor of Georg Stage, who died at the age of twenty-two. He was the son of Danish boat builder Frederik Stage. The original ship's figurehead, which portrays the young Georg Stage, was transferred to the ship, which now carries his name.

Georg Stage is primarily engaged in training young men and women for careers in maritime service. Under the administrative office of the Georg Stage Memorial Foundation, the ship provides an environment where "young people can acquire practical maritime skills at sea in situations where teamwork and mutual respect are essential; after which they can decide if life at sea will suit them."

Measuring a trim 178 feet from bowsprit to stern, she is the smallest fully rigged ship in the world.

SCANTLINGS
Length overall: 178'
Beam: 27' 6"
Draft: 13'
Hull: Iron plates
Rig: Ship
Year built: 1935
Home port: Copenhagen
Flag: Denmark

GLADAN AND FALKEN

These twin schooners were built in the same yard and according to the same plans in 1947.
Differentiated only by their sail numbers, S01 for *Gladan* and S02 for *Falken,* these two vessels
train future officers of the Swedish royal navy as they have since their commissioning.

SCANTLINGS
Length overall: 129'
Beam: 23'
Draft: 13' 9"
Hull: Steel
Rig: Schooner
Year built: 1947
Home port: Karlskrona
Flag: Sweden

GLORIA

Built to train future officers of the Colombian navy, *Gloria* recalls the great sail training barque of the 1930s, though she was one of four barques built during the 1960s and 1970s at the famous Astilleros y Talleres Celaya shipyard in Bilbao, Spain.

The concept of a training ship was promoted by three influential Colombian leaders: naval commander Admiral Orlando Lemaitre Torres; defense minister General Gabriel Rebeiz Pizarro; and project director Commander Benjamin Alzate Reyes. After her keel was laid in 1967, *Gloria* was completed in 1968. General Rebeiz died before the ship was christened, and as a gracious tribute to his efforts, to ensure that this important project reached completion, the vessel was named Gloria, for his wife, Gloria Zawadsky de Rebeiz.

Gloria carries a crew of ten officers, a professional crew of fifty, and sixty to seventy-five cadets on her extensive training cruises in the north and south Atlantic.

SCANTLINGS
Length overall: 249'
Beam: 34' 8"
Draft: 16' 4"
Hull: Steel
Rig: Barque
Year built: 1968
Home port: Cartegna
Flag: Colombia

SCANTLINGS
Length overall: 293'
Beam: 39'
Draft: 15' 6"
Hull: Steel
Rig: Barque
Year built: 1958
Home port: Kiel
Flag: Germany

GORCH FOCK II

Built from the same plans and in the same shipyard (Blohm & Voss in Hamburg, Germany) as the original, *Gorch Fock II* boasts contemporary safety features and the latest navigational equipment. She is an eminent replacement for her namesake (now the training vessel *Tovarishch* from Ukraine). Since her launch in 1958, *Gorch Fock II* has logged thousands of nautical miles in her twice-yearly voyages and has hosted more than ten thousand cadets for training cruises.

The barque is named for a popular German writer of sea stories, Hans Kinau (1880–1916), who used the pseudonym Gorch Fock (*fock* means "foresail" in German). Kinau became part of the romantic mythology of the sea when he perished aboard the cruiser *Weisbaden*, which was sunk during the Battle of Jutland on May 31, 1916.

Gorch Fock II is a proud symbol of Germany's distinguished sailing and shipbuilding traditions.

GÖTHEBORG

One of the largest wooden sailing ships in the world is also one of the newest members of the international fleet. The East Indiaman *Götheborg* is a replica of the ship of the same name that sank in 1745. Loaded with trade goods after her third voyage to Asia, *Götheborg* foundered after hitting a rock. The crew was saved and enough of the cargo was recovered to pay for the voyage and still leave a profit.

In 1985 researchers found the location of the wreck and the idea of re-creating the original ship was born. The keel for the new ship was laid in 1995, and work proceeded using eighteenth-century methods and materials. *Götheborg* was launched in 2003, but her first sea trials had to wait until her rig was completed in 2005. On its first voyage, the ship will follow the route of her predecessor, sailing to China and back over the course of two years. Thereafter *Götheborg* will sail the world as an emissary of Sweden.

SCANTLINGS
Length overall: 192'
Beam: 36'
Draft: 17' 3"
Hull: wood
Rig: Ship
Year buit: 2005
Home port: Götheborg
Flag: Sweden

GREIF

The first vessel launched in the former German Democratic Republic in 1951, this brig was constructed and named in honor of then-chancellor of the GDR Wilhelm Pieck, in celebration of his 75th birthday. Pieck presented the ship to the youth of the nation, and she officially became a schoolship on August 2, 1951. *Wilhelm Pieck* represented eastern Germany in many of the maritime festivals of the 1960s and 1970s.

In 1990 *Wilhelm Pieck* underwent a comprehensive overhaul, at which time she was renamed *Greif.* The brig now operates out of her home port of Greifswald on the Baltic Sea and offers sail training programs to the youth of Germany and other Baltic nations.

SCANTLINGS
Length overall: 135'
Beam: 25'
Draft: 12'
Hull: Steel
Rig: Brigantine
Year built: 1951
Home port: Greifswald,
    Germany
Flag: Germany

GROSSHERZOGIN ELISABETH

Christened *San Antonio,* this vessel first slipped down the ways in 1909 at Alblasserdam, Germany. A North Sea and Baltic trader, she was designed to carry 600 tons of cargo in three holds. More notable is that she may hold the record as the first sailing ship equipped with a diesel engine. Her search for trade led to African and South American voyages. Fitted with an even larger engine, she was by 1936 a motor ship flying only auxiliary sails. She continued to trade until 1972, when she was converted to carry passengers in the Mediterranean and the Caribbean. Renamed *Ariadne,* a new deckhouse and wheelhouse were added, and her rig was restored.

Her third life began in 1981. Laid up in Piraeus, Greece, she was discovered by Capt. Horst Werner Janssen, who wanted her to serve a sail training ship in Elsfleth, Germany. Sailed by a volunteer crew, she arrived in Germany in 1982. Though damaged by a fire during her refit in 1983, she has been fully refurbished and is now operated by the county of Landkreis *Wesermarsch* as a sail training base for apprentice ship mechanics and ship masters studying at its nautical school.

SCANTLINGS
Length overall: 216'
Beam: 27'
Draft: 7'
Hull: Steel
Rig: Schooner
Year built: 1909
Home port: Elsfleth, Germany
Flag: Germany

SCANTLINGS
Length overall: 257'
Beam: 33'
Draft: 14' 6"
Hull: Steel
Rig: Barque
Year built: 1977
Home port: Guayaquil
Flag: Ecuador

GUAYAS

The figurehead of a giant Condor distinguishes *Guayas* of Ecuador from her sister ship, *Gloria* of Columbia. Built in Spain in 1977, *Guayas* was commissioned for the training of cadets and junior officers of the Ecuadorian Naval Superior School at Guayaquil. The school, which was founded by Simón Bolívar in 1822, is located on the River Guayas, from which the ship takes her name.

Guayas is home to the 63 trainees on each of her cruises, with an additional complement of 110 crew and officers. The Ecuadorian navy still considers sail training essential to developing a spirit of teamwork in the country's young sailors.

SCANTLINGS
Length overall: 200'
Beam: 27' 3"
Draft: 10' 6"
Hull: Steel
Rig: Barque
Year built: 1940
Home port: Öckerö,
    Sweden
Flag: Sweden

GUNILLA

The largest square-rigged barque sailing in Sweden is *Gunilla*. Originally built in 1940 as a cargo vessel, *Gunilla* had her three bermudian masts removed when she was converted to a motor ship in 1954.

In 1997 *Gunilla* carried her last cargo of grain and was acquired by the association Mot Bättre Vetande, or MBV, which also operates the vessels *Hawila* and *Astrid Finne*. She began her transformation to a barque under the watchful eyes of Managing Director Lennart Martinson. With rigging designed by Allan Palmer, naval architect for the *Linden* and *Albanus, Gunilla* began to take shape. She now operates as a secondary school, offering combined curriculums in social sciences and natural sciences.

HALF MOON

Based on original Dutch East India Company specifications, *Half Moon* is a replica of the vessel *Halva Maen,* sailed by Henry Hudson in 1609. That first exploratory voyage led to the establishment of Dutch settlements in New York, New Jersey, Connecticut, and Delaware, then known as "Nieu Nederlandt." The new *Half Moon* was completed in 1989 at Albany, New York, the northernmost point of which was reached by Henry Hudson on the river that now bears his name.

Operated and maintained by the New Netherland Museum, *Half Moon* offers sail training and maritime history programs for young people and adults. She is a frequent visitor to East Coast ports and maritime festivals.

SCANTLINGS
Length overall: 95'
Beam: 17' 6"
Draft: 8' 5"
Hull: Wood
Rig: Barque
Year built: 1989
Home port: Croton-on-Hudson,
  New York
Flag: United States

HARVEY GAMAGE

A typical coastal schooner, *Harvey Gamage* is a virtual sister vessel of *Bill of Rights*. Both are identified by their large mainsails as they visit the waters of the northeast Atlantic. *Harvey Gamage* is named for the distinguished master shipwright from Maine, Harvey Gamage. She is a beautiful tribute to the shipbuilder's art and an example of the coastal vessels that plied the waters of the east coast a century ago carrying commercial cargo.

For the twenty-first century her purpose has been redefined. Under the auspices of a new nonprofit foundation, the Schooner *Harvey Gamage* Foundation of Francestown, New Hampshire, the schooner provides educational programs which use the power of the sea and the challenge of the sailing ship to lead students of all ages to intellectual and personal growth. The *Harvey Gamage* Sea Education programs are structured adventure expeditions integrated with academic studies in marine science, literature, arts and humanities, math and history. During the fall and spring semesters, *Harvey Gamage* serves as a sailing classroom for the Ocean Classroom program run in conjunction with Proctor Academy. Open adult programs are available during the summer in New England waters and during mid-winter in Caribbean waters.

Harvey Gamage sails with a permanent crew of seven to ten members, along with twenty-five students.

SCANTLINGS
Length overall: 131'
Beam: 23' 6"
Draft: 10'
Hull: Wood
Rig: Schooner
Year built: 1973
Home port: Bath, Maine
Flag: United States

HAWAIIAN CHIEFTAIN

Recalling traditional topsail ketches of northern European coastal traders, the *Hawaiian Chieftain* enjoys the advantages of a modern shallow draft steel hull with a twin keel. Built in Lahaina, Hawaii, in 1988, the ship sails at a very low angle of heel, and with a draft of only six feet is able to navigate in shallow waters.

For many years *Hawaiian Chieftain* sailed in the company of *Lady Washington* in Pacific waters off California. In 2004, however, she was sold to an East Coast sailing program, but the transition proved a brief one. The Grays Harbor Historical Seaport Authority in Washington purchased her in 2005, and she returned to Pacific waters in 2006. She is again sailing with *Lady Washington* in education and sail training on the West Coast. In defense of her educational programs, *Hawaiian Chieftain* has been known to fire her "water balloon" cannons upon "foreign vessels of unknown origin" sailing too close to her rhumb line.

SCANTLINGS
Length overall: 103'
Beam: 22'
Draft: 5'
Hull: Steel
Rig: Topsail ketch
Year built: 1988
Home port: Westport, Washington
Flag: United States

HAWILA

A 121-foot traditional Baltic ketch, *Hawila* sails frequently to tall ship events in the Baltic and North Seas. She is typical of the many black-hulled Baltic traders that have been converted to serve in sail training programs for youngsters. Asked about the meaning of her name, one crew member claimed that *Hawila* was named for an accurate Swiss watch, though he admitted in passing that her name also had a biblical allusion. In the story of Genesis, the river that watered the garden of Eden branched into four streams afterward. The first branch encircled all the land of "Havilah . . . where the gold is." The gold of Havilah was frankincense.

Hawila's wooden hull was completed in 1935. She was purchased by her present owner, the sailing association Mot Bättre Vetande, in 1978 and was rebuilt into a school sailing ship by young people who volunteered their time. She finally began her career as a school sailing ship in 1984. Her season generally runs from 1 May until the end of October. About four hundred trainees, ages fourteen to eighteen, sail aboard *Hawila* each year.

SCANTLINGS
Length overall: 121'
Beam: 21' 6"
Draft: 10'
Hull: Wood
Rig: Ketch
Year built: 1935
Home port: Öckerö
Flag: Sweden

HIGHLANDER SEA

William Starling Burgess designed three America's Cup defenders, *Rainbow, Ranger,* and *Enterprise.* He also designed some of the fastest fishing schooners in the U.S.: *Columbia,* the last Burgess boat to compete in the International Fisherman's cup races; *Mayflower;* and *Puritan.* Burgess's plans for *Highlander Sea* most resemble *Puritan,* but it is thought that she was intended to succeed *Columbia* and race against Canada's *Bluenose.*

Instead of fishing the Grand Banks, *Highlander Sea*—launched in 1924 and christened *Pilot*—began her career with the Boston Harbor Pilot Association, carrying pilots to ships entering Boston Harbor. After nearly four decades, *Pilot* was sold to a group that intended to sail her on a world circumnavigation. She was rerigged as a full gaff topsail schooner, but after reaching the South Pacific in 1976, she was purchased by Norman Paulsen to carry marine biology classes in California and renamed *Star Pilot.* Secunda Marine Service in Nova Scotia, Canada, purchased the boat in 1998, refitted her for sail training, and renamed her *Highlander Sea.*

Acheson Ventures purchased the vessel in 2002, and she became the flagship of Port Huron, Michigan, where she provides educational and youth development programs, as well as serving in the role of ambassador of the City of Port Huron throughout the Great Lakes.

SCANTLINGS
Length overall: 154'
Beam: 25' 2"
Draft: 14'
Year built: 1924
Hull: Wood
Home port: Port Huron, Michigan
Flag: United States

HOSHI

With elegant sheer lines and rigging more typical of a private yacht, *Hoshi* displays her lineage as a Camper & Nicholson design. After a number of private owners, she became the flagship of the Island Cruising Club (ICC) of Devon in 1958. For close to sixty years ICC has provided sail training and adventure cruises in and around England and neighboring waters with *Hoshi* and other vessels.

Hoshi, Japanese for "shooting star," has accommodations for twelve, including the skipper, mates, and cook.

SCANTLINGS
Length overall: 86'
Beam: 14' 2''
Draft: 8' 6''
Hull: Wood
Rig: Schooner
Year built: 1909
Home port: Salcombe, England
Flag: United Kingdom

INLAND SEAS

Inland Seas is a floating classroom outfitted with scientific equipment that enables students to study the Great Lakes ecosystem. The schooner is equipped with state-of-the-art navigational instruments and is a U.S. Coast Guard–certified passenger vessel. *Inland Seas* is staffed by a professional crew of mariners and educators.

SCANTLINGS
Length overall: 80'
Beam: 17'
Draft: 7'
Hull: Steel
Rig: Schooner
Year built: 1994
Home port: Suttons Bay, Michigan
Flag: United States

SCANTLINGS
Length overall: 110' 9"
Beam: 21' 9"
Draft: 11'
Hull: Wood
Rig: Brigantine
Year built: 2002
Home port: Los Angeles,
  California
Flag: United States

IRVING JOHNSON AND EXY JOHNSON

The twin brigantines *Irving Johnson* and *Exy Johnson* are named for the famed husband-and-wife sailing couple Irving (1905–1991) and Electra (1909–2004) Johnson, who circumnavigated the globe in their schooner *Yankee* and helped to instill a combination of idealism and youth that has become the basis of today's sail training programs.

The state-of-the-art brigantines were built by paid shipwrights and volunteers under the supervision of Master Builder Allen Rawl at the Brigantine Boatworks, Los Angeles Maritime Museum's boatyard. Each brig features an onboard laboratory, a library, and conference areas.

The Brigantine Boatworks and the twin brigs were created for the Los Angeles Maritime Institute's successful sail training program, TopSail, which teaches youth the skills needed to live healthy and successful lives.

ISKRA

Iskra, which in Polish means "spark" (as in "to spark a flame"), is named for an historically important Polish schooner of the early twentieth century. The first *Iskra* was a wooden, three-masted schooner that trained more than four thousand officers for the Polish navy in her fifty years of service, from 1927–77. The new *Iskra* carries the name ORP *Iskra* (Officers Reserve of Poland) in honor of the Westerplattes Heroes Naval Academy of Gdynia which she represents.

Another of the many vessels designed by Zygmunt Choren, *Iskra* proudly flies the navy ensign and represents the Republic of Poland on official visits.

SCANTLINGS
Length overall: 161'
Beam: 26'
Draft: 11' 6"
Hull: Steel
Rig: Barquentine
Year built: 1982
Home port: Gdynia
Flag: Poland

JAMES CRAIG

One of the oldest cargo vessels in the world still sailing, *James Craig* was built in the late nineteenth century at the Bartram Haswell & Company yards in England. After many ownership transfers and a brief stint servicing the South Pacific, she was rescued and relaunched in Tasmania in 1972–1973. In 1981 she was towed to Sydney and spent the next two decades undergoing a comprehensive restoration. The *James Craig* was completed in 2001 and set sail once again.

She is the proud flagship of the Sydney Heritage Fleet and an active presence in Sydney Harbor at the Sydney Maritime Museum.
She proudly serves as Sydney's goodwill ambassador to the sea!

SCANTLINGS
Length overall: 230'
Beam: 31' 2"
Draft: 12' 2"
Hull: Iron and cement
Rig: Barque
Year built: 1874
Home port: Sydney,
   Australia
Flag: Australia

SCANTLINGS
Length overall: 106'
Beam: 21'
Draft: 10' 6"
Hull: Wood
Rig: Brigantine
Year built: 1957
Home port: Leith, Scotland
Flag: United Kingdom

JEAN DE LA LUNE

Built as a motor trawler in 1957, *Jean de la Lune* served as part of the tuna fleet out of the Azores for a number of years. In the mid-1970s she was bought and refurbished in Colchester, England. She emerged as a staysail schooner and served briefly in the charter trade.

In 1988 she was acquired by her present owner, John Reid, who envisioned her as a square-rigger. Working with a team of volunteers, Reid spent six years completing the arduous conversion of *Jean de la Lune* to a brigantine.

In 1995 she was the host vessel for the tall ship regatta in Edinburgh, or, more precisely, Leith, Scotland.

JEANIE JOHNSTON

The recreation of *Jeanie Johnston* commemorates the emigration of Irish people from their homeland to North America as they sought to escape the Great Famine of the 1840s. Between 1847 and 1858, the original *Jeanie Johnston* carried thousands of emigrants from southwest Ireland to ports in the United States and Canada. With a crew of seventeen, she carried a full complement of two hundred passengers. Unlike the infamous "coffin ships," however, *Jeanie Johnston* made sixteen trips without the loss of a single life.

Dedicated in the spring of 1998, the "dream rebuilt" was realized only after overcoming numerous difficulties, from fund-raising and locating adequate timber to finding skilled shipwrights. On her maiden voyage, *Jeanie Johnston* plans an extended voyage from Ireland across the Atlantic, up the eastern seaboard, down the St. Lawrence River to the Great Lakes.

SCANTLINGS
Length overall: 176'
Beam: 26'
Draft: 12' 4"
Rig: Barque
Hull: Irish oak
Year built: 1999
Home port: Dublin
Flag: Ireland

JENS KROGH

Built in 1899 at Frederikshaven near the northern tip of Denmark, *Jens Krogh* now calls Ålborg, Denmark, her home port. Converted from a fishing vessel, *Jens Krogh* trains young Danish boys and girls in the art of sailing and in the marine sciences.

Called *Ulla Vita* before she was acquired in 1973 by the FDF Skøreds (the Danish sea scouts), the group restored and then renamed her *Jens Krogh*.

SCANTLINGS
Length overall: 80'
Beam: 16' 6"
Draft: 6' 10"
Hull: Wood
Rig: Ketch
Year built: 1899
Home port: Ålborg
Flag: Denmark

JOHANN SMIDT

Built at Amsterdam's Cammenga shipyard in 1974 and christened *Eendracht,* this modern schooner served as the first sail training ship for Holland's Het Zeilend Zeeschip. Designed as a training ship for young people, she participated in regattas and crossed the Atlantic. Her success led to the construction of a larger training ship, and, in 1989, *Eendracht* was sold to Clipper Deutsches Jugendwerk zur Sees in Hamburg, Germany. Renamed to honor Johann Smidt, a nineteenth-century lord mayor of Bremen, she continues her role as a successful sail training ship with an extensive cruising program in the Baltic and the Mediterranean.

SCANTLINGS
Length overall: 118'
Beam: 26' 6"
Draft: 12'
Hull: Steel
Rig: Schooner
Year built: 1974
Home port: Bremen,
  Germany
Flag: Germany

SCANTLINGS
Length overall: 76'
Beam: 15'
Draft: 11'
Hull: Wood
Rig: Cutter
Year built: 1913
Home port: Wiltshire,
    United Kingdom
Flag: United Kingdom

JOLIE BRISE

Built in 1913 in Le Havre, France, her speed under sail, as well as her unique service, ensure *Jolie Brise* an important place in the annals of sailing history. She won the first of the famous Fastnet Races in 1925 and went on to win the race again in 1929 and 1930. *Jolie Brise* was also the last vessel to deliver the Royal Mail under sail.

Jolie Brise is now operated jointly by Dauntsey's School Sailing Club and the Exeter Maritime Museum. With her legend already secure, *Jolie Brise* trains young people to meet the challenges of traditional sailing and marine life. Her extensive sailing program includes a transatlantic crossing during the year 2000.

SCANTLINGS
Length overall: 370'
Beam: 43'
Draft: 22' 6"
Hull: Steel
Rig: Topsail schooner
Year built: 1927
Home port: Cadiz
Flag: Spain

JUAN SEBASTIAN DE ELCANO

This graceful four-masted topsail schooner is one of the longest tall ships in the world and measures 370 feet long overall. *Juan Sebastian de Elcano* is officially the training ship for the midshipmen and ensigns of the Spanish navy.

The schooner is named in honor of Juan Sebastian de Elcano, captain of Ferdinand Magellan's last exploratory fleet. The captain returned to Seville, Spain, on 6 September 1522. The ship also carries the de Elcano coat of arms—a terraqueous globe and the motto "Primus Circumdedisti Me" (first to circumnavigate me)—which Emperor Charles I conferred on de Elcano after he returned to Spain having completed Magellan's global expedition.

Built in Cadiz, Spain, in 1927, the ship's hull was designed by the Echevarrieta y Larriñaga shipyard of Cadiz. Her rigging and sails were planned by the English sailmaker Nicholson. Both designs were used twenty-five years later to build the Chilean sail training vessel *Esmeralda* in 1952–1954.

Juan Sebastian de Elcano also honors four previous sail training vessels—*Bianca, Almansa, Asturias,* and *Nautilus*—by designating her masts with their names.

KAISEI

Built in Gdansk, Poland, *Kaisei,* the Japanese word for "ocean planet," served as Japan's first civilian sail training vessel. Her maiden voyage in 1992 included a circumnavigation of the British Isles as a tribute from one island nation to another. In 2005 *Kaisei* was acquired by the Ocean Institute, a nonprofit organization founded in 1979 by a group of international sailors, educators, and conservationists. The institute's mission is to teach maritime arts and sciences, and to explore and work to preserve the world's oceans. *Kaisei* will introduce crews of international students to the ocean environs of the Pacific, sailing from the southern coast of California.

SCANTLINGS
Length overall: 151'
Beam: 25'
Draft: 11' 2"
Hull: Steel
Rig: Brigantine
Year built: 1991
Home port: Sausalito, California
Flag: United States

KALIAKRA

Completed in 1984, *Kaliakra* trains future officers for the Bulgarian navy and is a sister ship to *Iskra*. Her home port is Varna on the Black Sea, although she has been a frequent participant in European and American tall ship gatherings. As initially rigged, only four yardarms crossed her foremast because of variations in deck thickness that affected the height of the foremast. Since her refitting in 1992, however, she carries five yardarms in her barquentine configuration. Her figurehead is a stylized version of a Bulgarian mythological figure.

SCANTLINGS
Length overall: 159'
Beam: 27'
Draft: 11'
Hull: Steel
Rig: Barquentine
Year built: 1984
Home port: Varna
Flag: Bulgaria

SCANTLINGS
Length overall: 139'
Beam: 24' 11"
Draft: 12' 2"
Hull: Wood
Rig: Ship
Year built: 1997/98
Home port: Wilmington,
  Delaware
Flag: United States

KALMAR NYCKEL

One of the newest additions to the fleet of international tall ships, *Kalmar Nyckel* was built in Wilmington, Delaware, and commissioned in 1998. She is a replica of the first Swedish ship to carry immigrants to America in 1638. The original *Kalmar Nyckel* brought several groups of Swedish, Finnish, Dutch, and Russian passengers to the shores of the Christina River in what is now Delaware.

The present *Kalmar Nyckel* is designated Delaware's official tall ship. Handled by professional staff and volunteers, she provides educational and sail training programs for young people sailing out of Wilmington, Delaware.

KAPITAN GLOWACKI

Found as an abandoned hull at the end of World War II, this restored and now well-traveled vessel worked originally as a German *Kriegsfishkutter,* a coastal fishing cutter. Rebuilt in 1951 as a gaff ketch, she served for decades as a school ship for young Polish fisherman. She underwent a second major refit in 1986 and was re-rigged as a brigantine for the Szkuner fishery shipyard in Poland.

During the Communist era, she was named in the Russian tradition for a hero of the State, one Henryk Rutkowski. After the democratization of Poland, the vessel was renamed for a revered faculty member of the maritime school in Gdynia, Wlodzimierz Glowacki, who died in 1995.

The trim brigantine also represents the Polish Yachting Association and serves as a sail training vessel for handicapped and drug-troubled youth. With her distinctive maroon sails, *Kapitan Glowacki* carries a professional crew of four and twenty-one cadet-trainees.

SCANTLINGS
Length overall: 94'
Beam: 21'
Draft: 10'
Hull: Wood and steel
Rig: Brigantine
Year built: 1944; refitted 1986
Home port: Gdynia
Flag: Poland

K A S K E L O T

Built in the J. Ring-Andersen yard of Svenborg, Denmark, *Kaskelot* underwent a major refit and rerigging in 1956 and emerged as the barque she is today. Built to serve the Greenland colonies as a supply ship, *Kaskelot* has been modified a number of times for her appearance in films. She has enjoyed starring roles as Capt. Michael Scott's *Terra Nova*, as Fried Nansen's *Fram,* and as *Hispaniola* in Robert Louis Stevenson's *Treasure Island*.

SCANTLINGS
Length overall: 153'
Beam: 25'
Draft: 12'
Hull: Wood
Rig: Barque
Year built: 1948
Home port: Jersey Island
Flag: United Kingdom

KHERSONES

Khersones is the fifth in a group of six full-rigged ships built in Gdansk, Poland during the 1980s. The other class A vessels are *Dar Mlodziezy* (1982), *Druzhba* (1986), *Mir* (1987), *Pallada* (1989), and *Nadezhda* (1992). *Khersones* is named for the ancient port of Khersone on the Black Sea. After upgrading and converting to accommodate cruise passengers, *Khersones* completed a circumnavigation. She now spends the summer months in European waters and books long, "Round Cape Horn," cruises during winter months.

SCANTLINGS
Length overall: 356'
Beam: 45' 9"
Draft: 21' 7"
Hull: Steel
Rig: Ship
Year built: 1987
Home port: Khersone
Flag: Ukraine

SCANTLINGS
Length overall: 376'
Beam: 46.1'
Draft: 23' 6"
Hull: Steel
Rig: Barque
Year built: 1926
Home port: St. Petersburg
Flag: Russia

K R U Z E N S H T E R N

This majestic, four-masted barque is the second largest working sailing ship in the world, surpassed in length only by Russia's other four-masted barque, *Sedov*. (*Kruzenshtern* is 376 feet long overall, while *Sedov* is 386 feet.) Both vessels are frequent visitors to festivals and regattas in Europe and America. *Kruzenshtern* is important historically as one of the last great deepwater cargo vessels of the twentieth century, with sailing traditions deeply rooted in the nineteenth century as it continues to sail in the twenty-first century.

Kruzenshtern, originally a vessel of the Flying P Line named *Padua,* was built for the F. Laeisz Co. in Hamburg, Germany. She made her last voyage as one of the Flying P cargo carriers in 1938–1939, leaving Bremen, Germany, for South America. During World War II, her hull was ignominiously converted for use as a barge. At the end of the hostilities she was transferred to the Soviet fleet and assigned to the Soviet Ministry of Fisheries as a training vessel. At that time, she was renamed *Kruzenshtern* to honor sailor, circumnavigator, and oceanographer Adam Johann Ritter von Kruzenshtern (1770–1846). Between 1959 and 1961, she underwent a major refit, and twin diesel engines were installed.

Following the transformation of the Soviet Union, she was registered in St. Petersburg, Russia, home of the famed oceanographer, and flies the Russian flag. Due to her particular history and construction, she has received grants from Germany to underwrite her maintenance and recent major refits.

LADY ELLEN

This elegant topsail schooner was designed as a charter vessel by her owners, Lars and Lars-Erik Johansson, in 1982. Her rig was inspired by a 1909 trading schooner named *Ellen* that transported timber betwen Scandinavia and the United Kingdom in the early twentieth century.

After running charters in the West Indies for two years, *Lady Ellen* participated in the tall ship gathering in Quebec in 1984 to commemorate the 450th anniversary of Jacques Cartier's discovery of Canada. She was purchased by her present owner in 1993 and refitted with a new deckhouse and rig. *Lady Ellen* sails from the archipelago of Stockholm.

SCANTLINGS
Length overall: 163' 6"
Beam: 25' 6"
Draft: 13' 6"
Hull: Steel
Rig: Topsail schooner
Year built : 1982
Home port: Stockholm,
  Sweden
Flag: Sweden

LADY MARYLAND

"Pungy" schooners were an indigenous and plentiful craft on the waters of and around the Chesapeake Bay. Throughout the nineteenth century these colorful ships served to dredge oysters and to transport commercial goods between many small ports along the bay. To commemorate these vessels, the Living Classroom Foundation of Baltimore has constructed a full-sized, authentic representation of these turn-of-the-century tall ships and created the two-masted, gaff-rigged pungy schooner *Lady Maryland*. Her green and pink colors are traditional.

Along the eastern seaboard of the United States from Maryland to Maine, this floating classroom has engaged students and youth in the study of marine science, ecology, and sailing. Beyond sail training, participants aboard *Lady Maryland* can learn everything from vocational skills, such as woodworking and marine mechanics, to such traditional classroom subjects as math and science. In addition, curricula have been developed for the study of the Chesapeake Watershed, the marine life in surrounding estuaries, and the natural resources of the area.

Lady Maryland also participates in programs with the Living Classroom's Maritime Institute, which is working toward the restoration of Maryland's historic skipjack fleet. Her educational programs are supported by private corporations, the city of Baltimore, and the state of Maryland.

SCANTLINGS
Length overall: 104'
Beam: 22'
Draft: 7'
Hull: Wood
Rig: Schooner
Year built: 1986
Home port: Baltimore, Maryland
Flag: United States

LADY NELSON

This petite vessel is a replica of the nineteenth-century brig named to honor the wife of England's greatest naval hero, Horatio Nelson (1758–1805). The original *Lady Nelson*, built in 1798–1799, left England in early 1800 for a ten-month voyage of discovery to Australia. She was the first vessel to sail through the Bass Strait from west to east, and from 1803 to 1804 she helped to establish the first European settlement on the Derwent River in Van Diemen's Land, now known as Tasmania.

Plans for the new *Lady Nelson* were begun in 1983 by the Tasmanian Sail Association to coincide with the centennial of the original vessel. In 1986, the first timber was cut and the keel was laid. Two years later, *Lady Nelson* was launched. Financial difficulties plagued the vessel until 1996, when the Friends of *Lady Nelson* was formed to take over the fiscal operation of the ship. Since that time, *Lady Nelson* has been engaged in sail training programs and based in Hobart, Tasmania.

SCANTLINGS
Length overall: 52' 8"
Beam: 17' 7"
Draft: 9'
Rig: Brig
Hull: Wood
Year built: 1987–1988
Home port: Hobart, Tasmania
Flag: Tasmania

SCANTLINGS
Length overall: 112'
Beam: 22'
Draft: 11'
Hull: Wood
Rig: Brig
Year built: 1989
Home port: Aberdeen, Washington
Flag: United States

LADY WASHINGTON

In 1787 Capt. Robert Gray sailed the ranging tender *Lady Washington*, together with *Columbia Rediviva*, from Boston, Massachusetts, on the first exploration of the uncharted waters of America's Pacific Northwest. The voyage led to the "discovery" and naming of Oregon's Columbia River and Gray's Harbor in Washington. On a later voyage, *Lady Washington* was the first ship to fly the American flag in Japan.

The current *Lady Washington* is a full-scale reproduction that duplicates the original to the extent that historical records and U.S. Coast Guard regulations permit. She is the largest square-rigged sailing vessel on the Pacific coast and among other statistics boasts more than three miles of traditional rope rigging. Built primarily from old-growth Douglas fir, *Lady Washington* was launched in 1989. She is a frequent visitor to harbors and maritime festivals up and down the Pacific Northwest and sails from Seattle during the summer months. She serves as the flagship of Grays Harbor Historical Seaport Authority in Aberdeen, Washington.

SCANTLINGS
Length overall: 64'
Beam: 14' 6"
Draft: 4' 9"
Rig: Gaff schooner
Hull: Wood
Year built: 1926
Home port: Seattle,
 Washington
Flag: United States

LAVENGRO

Built as the *Helen* in Back Bay, Mississippi, in 1927, *Lavengro* is a traditional gaff-rigged Biloxi schooner. Constructed of cypress planking with a yellow pine centerboard by noted shipwright Jack Covacavich, *Lavengro* joined the fleet of "White Winged Queens" sailing the Gulf of Mexico harvesting oysters and shrimp. During World War II she served the U.S. Coast Guard as a sail-training vessel. Later Thomas Bayne Denegre of New Orleans sailed her for pleasure, and then she worked carrying tourists out of Maui, Hawaii. Most recently she was donated to the Northwest Schooner Society, a nonprofit group dedicated to preserving classic wooden vessels. *Lavengro* now sails the waters of Puget Sound on scheduled day excursions and overnight voyages, as well as charter trips. In the Romany language of the Gypsies, *lavengro* means "wordmaster" and likely refers to the book *Lavengro and the Romany Rye* by George Borrow.

STS LEEUWIN II

STS *Leeuwin II* is named for the Dutch vessel that charted the southwestern corner of continental Australia in the seventeenth century. The Dutch word *leeuwin* means lioness. The effort to construct a sail training vessel for western Australia was aided by the enthusiasm and attention drawn to the region by Alan Bond's capture of the America's Cup in 1983. Completed in 1986, *Leeuwin II* participated in the defense of the America's Cup off Fremantle in 1987 as well as in Australia's bicentennial celebration in 1988.

Through most of the sailing season, STS *Leeuwin II* schedules ten-day sail training cruises for groups of young people. She is maintained and operated by the Leeuwin Ocean Adventure Foundation Ltd. of Fremantle.

SCANTLINGS
Length overall: 180'
Beam: 30'
Draft: 11'
Hull: Steel
Rig: Barquentine
Year built: 1986
Home port: Fremantle
Flag: Australia

SCANTLINGS
Length overall: 75'
Beam: 15' 2"
Draft: 4' and 8' 6"
Hull: Wood and epoxy
Rig: Schooner
Year built: 1993/94
Home port: Key West, Florida
Flag: United States

LEOPARD

Distinctive in plan and rigging, *Leopard* is the "dream schooner" of her designer and owner, Reuel Parker. She is built on the lines of the pilot schooner known as No. 17, which was cataloged by the French naval "constructor" and historian Jean Baptiste Marestier in 1821. The original design is similar to a Baltimore clipper, with a hull deeper aft than forward, sharply raked masts, and substantial sail area for extra speed. Parker combined the swift and seaworthy lines with a centerboard to create a vessel that is both stable in deepwater and can navigate in waters as shallow as 4 feet. *Leopard* is rigged with an overlapping lug-foresail and masts raked aft 10º from vertical.

Pilot schooners reflect an indigenous American design that evolved from the early schooners of the American Revolution to the Baltimore Clippers of the mid-nineteenth century. These vessels served as blockade runners, privateers, revenue cutters, slavers, men-of-war, and pilot schooners. Their designs promoted speed and weatherliness. Pilot schooners employed a simple rigging that permitted easy, single-handed sailing from the offshore Atlantic in all types of weather after discharging pilots to harbor-bound ships. The *Leopard* demonstrates these sailing characteristics, and her name, taken from the novel *The Snow Leopard,* by Peter Matthiessen, furthers her association with speed and agility.

SCANTLINGS
Length overall: 129'
Beam: 21'
Draft: 11'
Hull: Wood
Rig: Gaff topsail schooner
Year built: 1893; rebuilt 1923;
    restored 1993
Home port: New York, New York
Flag: United States

LETTIE G. HOWARD

The keel of this classic fishing schooner was laid down in the Essex, Massachusetts, shipyard of A.D. Story, where many of the schooners of the fishing fleets of Gloucester, Boston, and New York were produced. Built for Capt. Fred Howard, the schooner was named for his daughter, Lettie G. Howard, who celebrated her twenty-second birthday in 1893.

Built on the plan of Edward Burgess's schooner *Fredonia* of 1889, *Lettie G. Howard* proves the graceful lines, speed, and seaworthiness of the design.

For eight years, *Lettie G. Howard* fished out of Gloucester, Massachusetts. In 1901, she was sold for use off Mexico's Yucatan Peninsula. Rebuilt in 1923, her first auxiliary engine was added a year later. She continued to work in the Gulf of Mexico until 1968, when she was sold to the South Street Seaport Museum, New York.

In 1988 *Lettie G. Howard* was designated a National Historic Landmark. To mark her centenary in 1993, she was restored to her 1893 appearance. At the same time she was refitted to accommodate trainees on educational cruises.

SCANTLINGS
Length overall: 64'
Beam: 19'
Draft: 7' 6"
Hull: Steel
Rig: Gaff-rigged schooner
Year built: 1871
Home port: Camden, Maine
Flag: United States

LEWIS R. FRENCH

Billed as the oldest sailing vessel in American waters, *Lewis R. French* has operated on the Maine coast for more than 100 years. Built in Christmas Cove, Maine, in April 1871, she originally served as a freighter, delivering cargoes as diverse as lumber, firewood, bricks, granite, lime, and even Christmas trees to ports of the northeast.

Lewis R. French has been lovingly preserved by her owners, Captain Dan and Kathy Pease. In 1992, the schooner won recognition as a
National Historic Landmark, and was rechristened at the age of 125 on April 28, 1996.

LIBERTAD

This full-rigged ship represents the Argentine navy. At 356 feet in overall length, *Libertad* is one of the longest sailing ships in the world. A popular visitor to American and European ports and maritime festivals, *Libertad* participated in Operation Sails in 1964, 1976, 1986, and 1992. On one of her transatlantic crossings in 1966 she used all 28,500 square feet of her sails to set a new record—eight days and twelve hours—crossing the North Atlantic between Cape Race, Canada, and the English Channel, a record that still stands. Her figurehead is a sculpture that depicts Liberty, for which the ship is named.

SCANTLINGS
Length overall: 356'
Beam: 45' 3"
Draft: 21' 9"
Hull: Steel
Rig: Full-rigged ship
Year built: 1960
Home port: Buenos Aires
Flag: Argentina

LIBERTY CLIPPER

Purchased and relocated to Maine in 1995, *Liberty Clipper* is designed along the lines of nineteenth-century Baltimore clippers and recalls those popular vessels of the Chesapeake Bay. Originally, *Liberty Clipper* was a day charter vessel and operated for many years from Mystic, Connecticut. Then named *Mystic Clipper,* she was a familiar site on Long Island and Block Island Sounds.

In 1995 she was acquired by Sail, Inc., of Bath, Maine, and is one of two vessels offering programs collectively called Ocean Classroom.

SCANTLINGS
Length overall: 125'
Beam: 26'
Draft: 7' 6"
Hull: Steel
Rig: Schooner
Year built: 1983
Home port: Boston, Massachusetts
Flag: United States

LINDEN

Linden was built in Åland, Finland, in 1992. Based on the lines and fame of the original schooner named *Linden*, built in 1920, the new three-masted schooner recalls another century, although her safety features, including steel bulkheads, prepare her for the twenty-first century. The contemporary *Linden* was built by a group of sailing enthusiasts and artisans who sought to maintain the ship building tradition of the Åland Islands.

Linden is close to nature and her past. She is constructed of pine with Swedish tar between her planks. Her masts and bowsprit are of larch from the legendary forests of Kitee and Punkaharju in Finland. These "mast forests" were planted by Czar Alexander II in 1880 for future shipbuilding. Masts fashioned from these trees display characteristics common to the living trees: enduring strength.

SCANTLINGS
Length overall: 157' 6"
Beam: 28'
Draft: 9'
Hull: Wood
Rig: Schooner
Year built: 1992
Home port: Mariehamn
Flag: Finland

LORD NELSON

In 1978 the Jubilee Sailing Trust of Great Britain commissioned Colin Mudie to create a sail training vessel with specific characteristics and design features. The vessel was intended to provide a traditional sailing experience for able-bodied sailors while enabling physically challenged people to experience the wonder and awe of the sea. The special features of *Lord Nelson* include a design to maximize sailing stiffness and reduce heel in order to minimize roll; a flat deck and elevators between decks to allow the unobstructed passage of wheelchairs and other necessary equipment; a widened platform bowsprit that allows wheelchair access to set the jibs; and elimination of unnecessary clutter on deck to permit free movement.

Lord Nelson embodies the courage and fortitude she is intended to bring to her crews. She is named after Horatio Nelson, 1758–1805, the legendary admiral of the British fleet who was mortally wounded aboard his flagship, HMS *Victory*, at the Battle of Trafalgar. Nelson's smaller fleet defeated the Napoleonic fleet of French and Spanish warships that had threatened to invade England. *Lord Nelson* was christened on 4 July 1986 and has met the needs of a special population of sailors. The ship has been so successful that the Jubilee Sailing Trust has commissioned another vessel of similar design to be built, this time reviving traditional methods to construct a sail training vessel of wood.

SCANTLINGS
Length overall: 169' 6"
Beam: 28'
Draft: 13' 6"
Hull: Steel
Rig: Barque
Year built: 1986
Home port: Southampton
Flag: United Kingdom

LYNX

The original was built in Maryland and commissioned in July of 1812, during America's war with Great Britain, to carry goods with enough speed to elude British blockaders. On her first voyage, *Lynx* sailed to Bordeaux, France, returning with wine, stockings, and gloves. In 1813, the British captured *Lynx*. Renamed *Mosquidobit,* she served the Royal Navy until decommissioned in 1820.

Naval architect Melbourne Smith created a contemporary "interpretation" of the 1812 Baltimore Clipper schooner *Lynx*, which draws only 8½ feet of water. Launched in July 2001, the new *Lynx* was the first square-rigged vessel built in Rockport, Maine, since 1855. She is 25 feet shorter than the original, but only a foot narrower, which allows for a shallow draft but expansive sail plan.

The Lynx Educational Foundation teaches visitors about the War of 1812, the value of teamwork, and sail training. *Lynx* provides day sails, extended voyages, and charters.

SCANTLINGS
Length overall: 122'
Beam: 23'
Draft: 8' 6"
Hull: Wood
Rig: Topsail schooner
Year built: 2001
Home port: Newport Beach, California
Flag: United States

MADELINE

Built on the lines of a nineteenth-century Great Lakes fore-and-aft schooner, *Madeline* takes her name from a trading vessel that inspired her construction by volunteers of the Maritime Heritage Alliance in Traverse City, Michigan.

The original was built in Fairport, Ohio, during the winter of 1844–1845. Sailing out of Mackinac Island, *Madeline* probably carried barreled fish to the lower Great Lakes, returning with cargoes of salt used in the preservation process. During the summer of 1847 the lightship *Ocean* was in need of repairs, and *Madeline* took her place in the Straits of Mackinac. The $450 *Madeline* earned, however, was largely consumed by $300 in the repairs she required that September after a storm drove her aground on Beaver Island. During the winter of 1851 she served as a school ship for a group of young men who required attention to their "three R's." In 1862 Milwaukee became her home port, and that is probably where her career ended.

Begun in 1985 using traditional techniques and materials, the new *Madeline* was launched in 1990. At dockside, she serves as a Great Lakes maritime interpretation center. Under sail she is a training ship and goodwill ambassador representing Traverse City throughout the Great Lakes.

SCANTLINGS
Length overall: 82'
Beam: 16' 2"
Draft: 7' 7"
Rig: Schooner
Hull: Wood
Year built: 1990
Home port: Traverse City, Michigan
Flag: United States

MALABAR

Built in 1975, this gaff-rigged schooner with a ferro-cement hull was originally named *Rachel & Ebenezer*. She sailed in Atlantic waters until the 1990s, when she moved to the Great Lakes where her name was changed. She operated as part of the Traverse Tall Ship Company of Traverse City, Michigan, along with the schooner *Manitou*.

Malabar's success led her owners to commission a new and larger steel-hulled square-rigger. Sold to make way for the new vessel, *Malabar* has been purchased by Captain Steven Pagels and Downeast Windjammer Cruises of Maine. She has since been renamed *Calypso Explorer* and returned to Atlantic waters.

SCANTLINGS
Length overall: 105'
Beam: 21'
Draft: 8' 6"
Rig: Gaff topsail schooner
Hull: Ferro-cement
Year built: 1975
Home port: Cherryfield, Maine
Flag: United States

MARE FRISIUM

This striking charter vessel has a long history. Built in 1916, *Mare Frisium* worked as a fishing lugger until she was sold to a German shipping company in 1960. Her length was increased and for the next three decades *Mare Frisium* transported lumber from Scandinavia to England and Belgium. Laid up in 1995, she was converted to a three-masted topsail schooner and now serves as a charter and cruise vessel.

SCANTLINGS
Length overall: 170' 7"
Beam: 22'
Draft: 10'
Hull: Steel
Rig: Topsail schooner
Year built: 1919
Home port: Lemmer, Netherlands
Flag: The Netherlands

SCANTLINGS
Length overall: 154'
Beam: 26' 4"
Draft: 13' 5"
Hull: Wood
Rig: Topsail schooner
Year built: 1923
Home port: Rouen
Flag: France

MARITÉ

Built by Captain Gustave Ledun to fish the Grand Banks, *Marité* was "baptisé" in 1923 at Fécamp, France. In 1924 she returned from her first voyage carrying 100 tons of fish, but modern vessels soon rendered her obsolete. By 1933 *Marité* was sold to a Danish owner to fish off the Faeroe Islands.

During World War II, *Marité* was requisitioned by the British navy and harassed German shipping. In1954 she became an engine-driven vessel. In 1973 she was abandoned off the port of Tvoroyri. She waited in the mud until a group of Swedish sailors found her lines irresistible in 1978. By 1987, she was renovated to her original specifications and went to sea again.

After a decade of success as a charter and sail-training vessel in Stockholm, the *Marité* was sold to French owners. *Marité* now operates out of Saint Mâlo, on the northwest coast of France.

MARY E

Built in 1906 in Bath, Maine, *Mary E* has enjoyed home ports from Maine to Key West. She currently harbors in Greenport, New York.

For some 30 years, *Mary E* worked out of Block Island as a "swordfisherman" in the Block Island and Long Island Sounds.
After World War II she returned to Boothbay, Maine, where she underwent refitting in 1966, 1973, and 1987.

Mary E is a "bald-headed" gaff schooner, typical of thousands of coastal schooners that operated along the east coast of the United States in the nineteenth and twentieth centuries. Today she carries up to 25 passengers on day sails from the east end of Long Island and provides sail training programs for young people on the New York and Connecticut coasts of Long Island Sound.

SCANTLINGS
Length overall: 74' 8"
Beam: 14' 3"
Draft: 6' 4"
Hull: Wood
Rig: Gaff schooner
Year built: 1906
Home port: Greenport, New York
Flag: United States

MERCATOR

Mercator is a barkentine representing Belgium. She was built in 1932 at the Ramage & Ferguson yard in Leith, Scotland. As a sail training and cargo vessel on South American runs, she became the best known vessel under the Belgian flag. In 1956 she was one of the few vessels to participate in the first tall ship gathering sponsored by England's Sail Training Association.

Decommissioned in 1960, she served as a museum ship and attracted more than 3 million visitors. The year 1986 marked the beginnings of a long-term restoration and refitting, which has included renewing her wooden decks and overhauling her rigging. This enabled her to represent Belgium as the host flagship for the 1993 gathering of tall ships in Antwerp. Flying only a partial suite of sails, she led the parade of ships proudly before returning to Ostend, Belgium. There, ongoing restoration is returning her to full sail and service as a sail training vessel for the Belgian navy.

SCANTLINGS
Length overall: 257' 6"
Beam: 35'
Draft: 15' 6"
Hull: Steel
Rig: Barkentine
Year built: 1932
Home port: Ostend
Flag: Belgium

SCANTLINGS
Length overall: 358'
Beam: 45' 9"
Draft: 21' 7"
Hull: Steel
Rig: Ship
Year built: 1987
Home port: St. Petersburg
Flag: Russia

MIR

Mir, which is Russian for "peace," is one of four vessels completed in the Gdansk, Poland, shipyard for the former Soviet Union. She is a sister ship to the prototype vessel *Dar Mlodziezy* (1982) as well as *Druzhba* (1987), *Khersones* (1988), *Pallada* (1989), and *Nasheba* (1992). At 360 feet, *Mir* operates from the Marine Engineering College of St. Petersburg and offers courses in marine science and oceanography in addition to sail training.

SCANTLINGS
Length overall: 269'
Beam: 39'
Draft: 17'
Hull: Steel
Rig: Bark
Year built: 1938
Home port: Constanza
Flag: Romania

MIRCEA

The last of the quartet of sail school ships built in the Hamburg, Germany, yard of Blohm & Voss in the 1930s, *Mircea* is the flagship and training vessel of the Romanian navy. *Mircea* and her sister ships became the models for sailing vessels that incorporate a school for the training of naval and merchant marine officers. The concept was replicated in the school ships of Latin American countries and the *Dar Mlodziezy*–class vessels built in Gdansk in the past decade. *Mircea* is named for a fourteenth-century Romanian hero, Prince Mircea, who liberated the Black Sea coastline from the Turks and, in doing so, established Romania's maritime heritage.

SCANTLINGS
Length overall: 62'
Beam: 15'
Draft: 6' 6"
Hull: Ferro-cement
Rig: Gaff ketch
Year built: 1981
Home port: Chatham, Kent,
   United Kingdom
Flag: United Kingdom

MORNING STAR of REVELATION

Morning Star of Revelation offers programs that combine sail training and Christian-oriented fellowship at sea. In addition to summer programs in coastal waters, *Morning Star of Revelation* has also participated in the Cutty Sark tall ship races and plans on a multiple-port, five-month transatlantic voyage with several crew changes on the Atlantic side of the United States and Canada.

MYSTIC WHALER

Based on the design of traditional New England trading schooners, *Mystic Whaler* visits ports along the Atlantic coast on day sails and overnight cruises during the summer season. She makes lighthouse cruises that emphasize the picturesque guardians of the New England coast, and explores the islands of Long Island and Rhode Island Sounds. *Mystic Whaler* sails with a crew of five and accommodates thirty-eight guests.

SCANTLINGS
Length overall: 110'
Beam: 25'
Draft: 7' 6"
Hull: Steel
Rig: Schooner
Year built: 1967
Home port: Mystic, Connecticut
Flag: United States

NADEZHDA

With three notable predecessors, the current *Nadezhda* shares a history that spans more than two hundred years, which may in part be explained by her name, the Russian word for "hope."

Shortly after she became empress of Russia, Katherine II prompted a revitalization of the country's navy, and in July of 1764 the Admiralty Board moved to have a three-masted ship built to train naval cadets. This ten-gun frigate, the first *Nadezhda*, was launched in June of 1766 at St. Petersburg. After eight years of sail training, the poorly built *Nadezhda* was retired.

The second *Nadezhda* was a three-masted sloop built in Britain and purchased in 1803 by the Russian-American Co. She served as the flagship of the first Russian round-the-world voyage, a three-year scientific expedition completed in 1806. The ship was chartered in 1808 to carry cargo for an American company; however, she became trapped in ice off the coast of Denmark and was lost.

The most direct predecessor of the current ship is the twenty-four-gun frigate *Nadezhda,* which was launched in 1845 to provide sail training for Russia's naval college at St. Petersburg. She carried a crew of one hundred eighty-eight, including seventy-five trainees.

The current *Nadezhda* was built at the Gdansk Shipyard in Poland and launched in 1992. Square-rigged with a steel hull, she carries twenty-six sails. The last of the "Dar" class ships built at the yard, her sister ships include *Dar Mlodziezy, Druzhba, Mir, Kherson,* and *Pallada.*

SCANTLIINGS
Length Overall: 359'
Beam: 46'
Draft: 21' 6"
Rig: Ship
Hull: Steel
Year built: 1991
Home port: Vladivostok
Flag: Russia

SCANTLINGS
Length overall: 198'
Beam: 32' 6"
Draft 11'
Hull: Wood
Rig: Brig
Year built: 1988
Home port: Erie, Pennsylvania
Flag: United States

NIAGARA

The U.S. brig *Niagara* is a reconstruction of the relief flagship of Commodore Oliver Hazard Perry. On 10 September 1813, Perry led nine small ships, including *Niagara*, against a British squadron of six vessels in the Battle of Lake Erie at Put-in-Bay, Ohio. It proved to be a pivotal battle of the War of 1812 and secured the Northwest Territory, opened supply lines, and boosted the nation's morale. During the battle, Perry engaged the British ships *Detroit* and *Queen Charlotte*. After his flagship, *Lawrence*, was disabled, Perry transferred his command to the undamaged *Niagara* and hoisted his battle flag, which was inscribed with the motto, "Don't Give up the Ship."

Owned by the Pennsylvania Historical and Museum Commission, *Niagara* is a working vessel dedicated to presenting living history. Built in 1988 of wood, *Niagara* educates the public about the ships and sailors of the War of 1812. In addition, she is the official flagship of the Commonwealth of Pennsylvania and makes several goodwill appearances annually with a crew of forty, half of whom are volunteers.

NIPPON MARU II
AND KAIWO MARU II

These twin barques were built in 1984 and 1989 by the Institute of Sea Training in Japan to replace the *Nippon Maru* I and *Kaiwo Maru* I, built in the 1930s as sail training vessels and then used as demasted barges during World War II.

The original vessels were 318-foot barques; their modern 361-foot sisters incorporate the experience of earlier sail trainers and modern requirements.

The *Nippon Maru* II and *Kaiwo Maru* II are emissaries of culture and goodwill around the world for the Japanese people. Each barque carries 70, including officers and permanent crew members, and a cadet contingent of 120. Each has 36 sails, and, before the wind, the sail area is close to 30,000 square feet.

The *Kaiwo Maru* II was swept ashore by typhoon *Tokage* on October 20, 2004. All the trainees were rescued; the ship suffered extensive rig and hull damage. She was expected to resume sailing in 2006.

SCANTLINGS
Length overall: 361'
Beam: 46'
Draft: 22'
Hull: Steel
Rig: Four-masted barque
Years built: 1984 and 1989,
 respectively
Home port: Tokyo
Flag: Japan

NORDEN

One of the few nineteenth-century vessels sailing in the tall ship fleet, *Norden* is a sturdy Norwegian cutter that has sailed for more than a century. Built in Skonevig, Norway, in 1870, she served as a freight vessel on Norway's west coast until 1978.

Exceptionally thick oak beams and good Norwegian construction helped *Norden* endure high seas, wars, and various owners for more than 100 years. In 1978, work began to restore *Norden* to her original condition. While restored in a strictly traditional manner, modern technology was added to the ship to make each voyage safer and more enjoyable. Peter Fleck serves as *Norden's* talented captain.

SCANTLINGS
Length overall: 93'
Beam: 19' 6"
Draft: 8'
Hull: Wood
Rig: Cutter
Year built: 1870
Home port: Lubeck, Germany
Flag: Germany

NORFOLK

The skipjack *Norfolk* was built at Deal Island, Maryland, in 1900. Originally christened *George W. Collier*, she dredged oysters for many years, working under a still-applicable Maryland law that mandates that Chesapeake Bay oysters be harvested only by vessels under sail. Skipjacks were introduced in the bay in the mid-nineteenth century. They are distinguished by hulls with hard chines, large centerboards, sloop rigs, and foresails set on a bowsprit. They were a vital part of the bay's development and worked from Norfolk, Virginia, to Baltimore, Maryland. One of only a few surviving examples of skipjacks from the turn of the century, the *Norfolk* represents a significant part of the Chesapeake Bay's commercial fishing industry.

At the end of her working career, she was donated to the city of Norfolk and rechristened *Norfolk*. In 1990, she was rebuilt and refitted under the auspices of a grant to the city from the Dalis Foundation. She is now operated by the Norfolk Parks and Recreation Department in cooperation with qualified volunteers, Sea Scouts, and Nautical Adventures, Inc.

SCANTLINGS
Length overall: 71'
Beam: 15' 6"
Draft: 7' with centerboard
Hull: Wood
Rig: Skipjack
Year built: 1900
Home port: Norfolk, Virginia
Flag: United States

SCANTLINGS
Length overall: 93' 6"
Beam: 19'
Draft: 9' 6"
Hull: Wood
Rig: Ketch
Year built: 1942
Home port: Cognac,
   France
Flag: France

NOTRE DAME DES FLÔTS

Although *Notre Dame des Flôts* was built in 1942 in Gravelines, France, her design is based on a 1910 ketch-rigged herring boat, and she worked as a North Sea fishing trawler until 1974. Unable to compete with vessels of more modern design, she was laid up and intentionally sunk in Dunkerque's boat graveyard.

Two years later a group led by Jean Pierre Despres refloated her and spent seven years restoring and adapting her to become a passenger charter vessel.

In 1983 she sailed around the world. Now a widely traveled ambassador of French culture, *Notre Dame des Flôts* appears at maritime festivals from Halifax (1984) and Sail Osaka (1997), to the Cutty Sark tall ship races (1998).

OOSTERSCHELDE

Oosterschelde is further proof that well-founded boats have many lives. Built in 1918 as a Dutch schooner with a flared clipper bow and an overhanging bulwark at the stern, *Oosterschelde* worked as a cargo vessel. Sailing between Africa and Europe, she carried 400 tons of cargo, ranging from clay and bricks to salt herring and bananas.

In the 1930s the era of sail was largely over. *Oosterschelde*'s bowsprit and topmasts were removed, she was refitted with a larger diesel engine, and sold to a Danish company that renamed her *Fulgen*. She was sold again in 1954. Purchased by a Swedish firm, her masts were unstepped, she was rebuilt as a motor coaster and renamed *Sylvan*.

Finally in 1988, Dutchman Dick van Andel recognized her as the last vessel of her type and brought her home to be restored. Work began in 1990 in consultation with three maritime museums. Two years later, *Oosterschelde* was relaunched by Her Royal Highness Princess Margriet.

She now sails as a private charter and sail training vessel in waters worldwide. *Oosterschelde* also serves as a sea-going representative of the city of Rotterdam.

SCANTLINGS
Length overall: 167'
Beam: 25'
Draft: 10'
Hull: Steel
Rig: Topsail schooner
Year built: 1918
Home port: Rotterdam
Flag: The Netherlands

HMCS ORIOLE

Launched in June 1921, *Oriole* IV was the last in a series of vessels dating to 1880 that shared the swift-flying bird's name. Built for the commodore of Toronto's Royal Canadian Yacht Club, *Oriole* was designed by George Owen of New York as a ketch-rigged centerboard schooner appropriate for both racing and cruising. The Navy League of Canada in Toronto acquired *Oriole* IV at the start of World War II. She trained sea cadets on the Great Lakes until 1949, when she was moved to the Maritimes for the training of new seamen. Formally commissioned HMCS *Oriole* in 1952, she was assigned to Pacific waters in 1954, sailing by the Panama Canal to British Columbia to take up a new station as tender to the naval training ship HMCS *Venture*. Since she carries no winches, many hands and teamwork are essential to sail handling on *Oriole*. Her 2,500-square-foot genoa is dwarfed by the 7,700 square-foot spinnaker that flies on a 42-foot-long pole that is set with the hands of fifteen cadets. Known widely as the people's boat, *Oriole* is now the Canadian navy's longest serving ship.

SCANTLINGS
Length overall: 102'
Beam: 19'
Draft: 10'
Rig: Marconi ketch
Hull: Steel
Year built: 1921
Home port: Esquimalt, British Columbia
Flag: Canada

PACIFIC GRACE

The Grand Banks schooner is a special icon for Canadians. The vessel is pictured on the verso of every Canadian dime. When *Robertson II,* one of the last original Grand Banks schooners and an important Canadian maritime artifact, retired in late 1995, the decision was made to build a replacement. The lines were drawn and patterns made for what was to become the new *Pacific Grace.* It was the intention of the Sail and Life Training Society (SALTS) program to preserve the design and heritage of *Robertson II.*

Pacific Grace was launched on October 9, 1999, and commissioned on May 21, 2001, and the first school group came aboard for a trip just ten days later. *Pacific Grace* joined *Pacific Swift* as part of the SALTS fleet. She hosts regular coastal sail training programs and cruises for the group.

SCANTLINGS
Length overall: 130'
Beam: 22' 2"
Draft: 11'
Hull: Wood
Rig: Schooner
Year built: 1999–2000
Home port: Victoria, British Columbia
Flag: Canada

PACIFIC SWIFT

Built during Expo '86 in Vancouver, British Columbia, *Pacific Swift* is the flagship of the Sail and Life Training Society (SALTS) of Victoria, British Columbia. Along with another school vessel, *Robertson II, Pacific Swift* embarks on six-month educational journeys throughout the South Pacific.

Crafted from local timbers, Alaskan cedar, and Douglas fir, *Pacific Swift* was modeled after the eighteenth-century brig *Swift*. The original *Swift* was probably built in the Canadian Maritimes, suggested by the French fleur-de-lis which decorate her transom. She was captured by the British navy and hauled out in London in 1783 for a survey. She was described as a clipper packet brig. The "clipper" designation referred to her shape; it suggests that she was designed for speed. "Packet" referred to the merchant or commercial service in which she was engaged; and "brig" described her rigging, which allowed for downwind sailing, with her two masts of square sails and a fore-and-aft sail on the mainmast to allow for more maneuverability and speed when sailing into the wind. *Pacific Swift* has added a few more fore-and-aft sails to her rig as a topsail schooner to allow for more maneuverability.

SCANTLINGS
Length overall: 111'
Beam: 20' 6"
Draft: 10'
Hull: Wood
Rig: Topsail schooner
Year built: 1986
Home port: Victoria,
 British Columbia
Flag: Canada

SCANTLINGS
Length overall: 226'
Beam: 33'
Draft: 16'
Hull: Steel
Rig: Barquentine
Year built: 1934
Home port: La Maddalena,
    Sardinia
Flag: Italy

PALINURO

In her first incarnation, *Palinuro* enjoyed a long career fishing for cod on the Grand Banks. Built in Nantes, France, in 1933, she was known originally as *Commandant Louis Richard* and, later, as *Jean Marc Aline.*

Purchased in 1950 by the Italian navy, she was renamed after the helmsman in the Greek legend of Aeneas, a prince of Troy and son of Venus. Aeneas fled Troy after its destruction and sailed on a course toward Italy in search of a new homeland. Venus interceded with Neptune to allow Aeneas to reach his goal safely. Neptune agreed but exacted a life as ransom. Palinurus, the victim in this bargain, was drugged at Neptune's behest by Somnus, who then pushed the unlucky Palinurus overboard. True to his promise, however, Neptune ensured the safe arrival in Italy of Aeneas and his ship.

After an extensive refitting, in 1955 *Palinuro* began her new role as a sail training ship for future naval petty officers. Recently overhauled, *Palinuro*'s white-striped color scheme echoes the style of *Amerigo Vespucci,* the other Italian navy training vessel. Though she sails mainly in the Mediterranean, *Palinuro* participated in the 1998 Cutty Sark race between England and northern European ports.

SCANTLINGS
Length overall: 356' 4"
Beam: 45' 9"
Draft: 22' 4"
Hull: Steel
Rig: Full-rigged ship
Year built: 1989
Home port: Vladivostok
Flag: Russia

PALLADA

Pallada is the fifth ship of the *Dar Mlodziezy*–class built in Poland during the1980s. Unlike her white-hulled sisters, *Pallada* has a black hull with false gunports and resembles the great Russian barque *Kruzenshtern*. She is named for the Greek goddess Pallas Athena. She is owned by Dalryba, a conglomerate of fishing companies, and offers sail training to foreign marine-college cadets.

Though her home port is Vladivostok, which is on the far eastern coast of Russia, *Pallada* voyages widely. She visited the west coast of the United States in 1989 and Europe in 1991; participated in the European Columbus Regatta in 1992; completed a circumnavigation to celebrate the 500th anniversary of the Russian navy in 1996; and sailed in the 1997 Hong Kong to Osaka race.

Pallada sails with a complement of 143 cadets and a permanent crew of 56 officers, teachers, and professionals. With twenty-six sails and masts soaring 162 feet above the deck, *Pallada* combines traditional sail training with a modern maritime college curriculum.

PATRICIA DIVINE

Designed by Merritt Walter and built in 1987, *Patricia Divine* is named for her owner's daughter. Though constructed using modern materials, the schooner's lines are based on the plan for a nineteenth-century British Revenue cutter.

Operating from the Chesapeake Bay, *Patricia Divine* passed her sea trials with a cruise from her home port to Bermuda and back again. She is the only vessel to have sailed in all nine of the Great Chesapeake Bay Schooner Races, which are held annually in October.

Patricia Divine combines traditional lines with elegant interior detailing to ensure that her charter and sail training voyages are as comfortable as they are instructive. Built for the luxury charter trade, she is certified to carry twenty-five day passengers and six overnight guests.

SCANTLINGS
Length overall: 69' 6"
Beam: 14' 8"
Draft: 6' 6"
Hull: Steel
Rig: Topsail schooner
Year built: 1987
Home port: Annapolis, Maryland
Flag: United States

PICTON CASTLE

Picton Castle began her career as a trawler–mine sweeper. Built in 1928 at Cochrane's Shipbuilding in Selby, England, she was one of five vessels named after Scottish castles. She gained her first moment of fame when she was lauded as the liberator of Norway after arriving in the harbor of Bergen on the day after occupying Nazis had retreated in 1944. Thereafter, she served as a trawler-freighter in the North Sea until her transformation into an idealistic, twentieth-century traditional sailer.

Picton Castle was converted to a sailing barque in Lunenburg, Nova Scotia, and under the command of Capt. Daniel Morehead has become a widely traveled platform for a unique educational program that ties the sailing traditions of Nova Scotia to the islands of the South Pacific.

Having completed her first voyage to the Cook Islands, as part of a world circumnavigation, *Picton Castle* anticipates embarking on another extended voyage in early 2001.

SCANTLINGS
Length overall: 176'
Beam: 24'
Draft: 14' 6"
Rig : Barque
Hull: Steel
Year built: 1928; rebuilt, 1996–1997
Home port: Avatia, Raratonga
Flag: Cook Islands

PILGRIM AND SPIRIT OF DANA POINT

The schooner *Spirit of Dana Point* and the brig *Pilgrim* are integral parts of the maritime and educational program of the Ocean Institute. Together, these ships host more than 16,000 students annually and serve as sail training vessels during summer cruises along the California coast.

Pilgrim is a replica of Boston-based merchant firm Bryant & Sturgis's cargo trader that journeyed between New England and the California coast to bring commercial and mercantile goods from Boston to the west coast and then returned to New England with hides and raw products. Built at a cost of $50,000 in 1825, the original ship was the inspiration for Richard Dana's maritime classic *Two Years before the Mast*. Today's *Pilgrim* was built in 1945 as a three-masted Baltic trader in Denmark. Her rig was converted to a brig in 1975 in Lisbon, Portugal, and she arrived at Dana Point in September 1981.

Formerly known as *Pilgrim of Newport*, *Spirit of Dana Point* is a replica of a 1770s American privateer used during the Revolutionary War. Dennis Holland dreamed of recreating an eighteenth-century sailing vessel of the era when American fought for her independence. Using plans from the Smithsonian Institution, Holland began building the schooner in 1970. Thirteen years later, the coastal schooner was complete.

SCANTLINGS, *PILGRIM*
Length overall: 130'
Beam: 24' 6"
Draft: 9'
Hull: Wood
Rig: Brig
Year built: 1945
Home port: Dana Point, California
Flag: United States

SCANTLINGS, *SPIRIT OF DANA POINT*
Length overall: 118'
Beam: 25'
Draft: 10'
Hull: Wood
Rig: Schooner
Year built: 1983
Home port: Dana Point, California
Flag: United States

PIONEER

A workhorse of a vessel, *Pioneer* was originally an iron-clad sloop, designated to carry raw materials on the coastal waters of New Jersey, New York, and Pennsylvania. She worked first for the Pioneer Iron Company, transporting sand to its main foundry in Chester, Pennsylvania. After being refitted with a more traditional schooner rig in 1895, *Pioneer* continued to transport coal, lumber, bricks, and eventually oil as a tanker until 1956.

In 1955, at the end of a working career of seven decades, she was sold to Russell Grinell of Gloucester, Massachusetts, who began an arduous reconstruction of her hull using steel plating and restored *Pioneer* to a traditional sailing rig. Upon his death in 1970 she was donated to New York's South Street Seaport, where *Pioneer* has continued to exemplify the nineteenth-century sailing traditions of the mid-Atlantic seaboard.

SCANTLINGS
Length overall: 102'
Beam: 21' 6"
Draft: 4' 8"
Hull: Iron and steel
Rig: Schooner
Year built: 1885
Home port: New York, New York
Flag: United States

SCANTLINGS
Length overall: 72'
Beam: 15'
Draft: 8'
Hull: Steel
Rig: Brigantine
Year built: 1973
Home port: Toronto, Ontario
Flag: Canada

PLAYFAIR

Playfair is the second of two steel-hulled brigantines owned and operated by Toronto Brigantine, Inc., of Toronto, Ontario. She was built in 1973 to accommodate the growing number of youth participating in the group's sail training programs and was given her name by Queen Elizabeth II.

Playfair and her sister ship, *Pathfinder,* have offered educational and sail training programs to more than 15,000 young people on the Great Lakes since 1964. The peer-led training programs are run by a crew of youth between the ages of 14 and 18 and emphasize leadership, teamwork, and responsibility in the operation and sailing of a ship. During the summer programs, the two ships sail more than 4,000 miles around the Great Lakes.

POGORIA

Pogoria holds the distinction of being the first completed design for a square-rigger by Polish naval architect Zygmunt Choren. Built for the Steel Workers Union in 1980, *Pogoria* has served as the background for a movie and as a floating classroom for West Island College of Quebec, Canada. She is now the flagship of the Polish Sail Training Association in Gdansk.

Pogoria's hull design served as the model for three other vessels: *Iskra* for the Polish navy, *Kaliakra* for the Bulgarian navy, and *Oceania,* a specially rigged oceanographic research vessel from Gdynia, Poland.

SCANTLINGS
Length overall: 154'
Beam: 26'
Draft: 11' 6"
Hull: Steel
Rig: Barkentine
Year built: 1980
Home port: Gdynia
Flag: Poland

PRIDE OF BALTIMORE II

Pride of Baltimore II is a topsail schooner built to the lines of a nineteenth-century Baltimore clipper. With her clipper bow, exaggerated bowsprit, and the distinct rake to her masts, *Pride of Baltimore II* is a living part of a past era. Her mission now, however, is to carry knowledge and teach discipline to the crews of youthful students who crowd her deck. She is owned by the state of Maryland and is operated by *Pride of Baltimore,* Inc.

Pride of Baltimore II sails as a goodwill ambassador for the state of Maryland and for the city and port of Baltimore. She has successfully completed voyages to the West Coast (including Alaska and Hawaii), South America, and to European waters. She sails with two rotating captains and a crew of eleven.

SCANTLINGS
Length overall: 170'
Beam: 26'
Draft: 12' 4"
Hull: Wood
Rig: Topsail schooner
Year built: 1988
Home port: Baltimore, Maryland
Flag: United States

PRINCE WILLIAM

The second of two brigs built for the Sail Training Association as replacements for their aging schooners, *Malcolm Miller* and *Sir Winston Churchill, Prince William* was completed in 2001. Her name was approved by the Prince of Wales and reinforces the link between Britain's Royal Family and sail training for youth. The funding for her construction, which cost £5.5 million, came largely from the Sport England Lottery Fund as well as corporate and private donors.

Prince William can accommodate 48 trainees and a small crew. The brig was built at the Appledore Shipyard in north Devon, England.

SCANTLINGS
Length overall: 195'
Beam: 32' 6"
Draft: 14' 8"
Hull: Steel
Rig: Brig
Year built: 2001
Home port: London,
  England
Flag: United Kingdom

PROVIDENCE

Providence is a replica of one of America's most historic vessels, the sloop *Katy*. She was the first vessel selected for the Continental navy and the first command of John Paul Jones, father of the America's navy. As a Revolutionary War vessel, she carried twelve cannons and is credited with having captured or sunk more than forty foreign fighting vessels. She was the first vessel to land amphibious troops, the American marines, on foreign soil.

Providence is maintained and operated by a nonprofit foundation, Seaport '76. She was built in time for the bicentennial celebrations of 1976 and since then has logged thousands of miles representing the nation, the state of Rhode Island, and the city of Newport at domestic and international maritime celebrations.

SCANTLINGS
Length overall: 110'
Beam: 20'
Draft: 10'
Hull: Fiberglass and wood
Rig: Square-sail sloop
Year built: 1976
Home port: Newport, Rhode Island
Flag: United States

PROVIDENT

Built in 1924 on the Dart River in Devon, England, *Provident* replaced a vessel of the same name sunk during World War I. She was privately owned until 1951, when she became the founding vessel of the Island Cruising Club (ICC). She was one of the vessels to participate in the 1956 English Tall Ships races that sparked a revival of interest in ships of the past.

Provident underwent a major refit in the 1980s. Relaunched in 1991, she continued to serve the ICC until 1999. Since then she has sailed from Brixham, England, under the aegis of the Trinity Sailing Foundation. Distinguished by her tan bark sails and green hull, *Provident* is available for cruises, charters, and sail training programs.

SCANTLINGS
Length overall: 92'
Beam: 18'
Draft: 8' 9"
Rig: Brixham Trawler
Hull: Wood
Year built: 1924
Home port: Brixham, Devon
Flag: United Kingdom

SCANTLINGS
Length overall: 91'
Beam: 20'
Draft: 4' 6"
Hull: Wood
Rig: Gaff schooner
Year built: 1984
Home port: New Haven,
   Connecticut
Flag: United States

QUINNIPIACK

A two-masted, gaff-rigged centerboard schooner, the *Quinnipiack* was designed along the lines of a Biloxi, Mississippi, cargo and oyster schooner. These shallow draft schooners carried freight or dredged for shellfish along the Mississippi Gulf coast in the late 1900s.

The *Quinnipiack* was built in Milbridge, Maine, by Capt. Steve Pagels from the design of Howard I. Chappelle and sailed as a charter schooner out of Bar Harbor, Maine. The vessel is noteworthy in that she is almost entirely built from the wood of native Maine "hackmatack," the Algonquian Indian name for a type of North American larch. In 1990 she was purchased by Schooner, Inc., to serve as a platform for environmental education programs. Her design is ideal for the coastal and estuarine studies she pursues.

R. TUCKER THOMPSON

Robert Tucker Thompson was an entrepreneurial Californian who loved to sail. Though trained as a teacher, sailboats were his real passion. It is likely that Tucker, as he preferred to be called, inspired Ralph Whitford to arrange for the purchase of the first sail training vessel for Sea Scouts in southern California.

In 1972, Thompson and his family decided to immigrate to New Zealand, where, among other projects, he determined to build a boat. Thompson laid the keel and framed the hull in his garden. He had nearly finished attaching steel plates to the frames in 1978 when heart disease led to his untimely death at age 47. Work on the boat devolved to Tucker's son Tod and his friend Russell Harris. Built in Mangawhai, New Zealand, *R. Tucker Thompson* was finally launched in 1985.

Based on the design of traditional halibut fishing boats from the American northwest, she is a gaff-rigged topsail schooner that has proved her plan to be fast, sea kindly, and easy to handle. Though made of steel, her deck is overlaid with New Zealand kwila wood, with masts and spars from Oregon, so while she looks and operates much like a nineteenth-century vessel, she enjoys the advantages of contemporary construction. *R. Tucker Thompson* sails in New Zealand waters on day trips and charters, although she is licensed for offshore sailing and has circumnavigated the globe.

SCANTLINGS
Length overall: 85'
Beam: 16'
Draft: 8' 6"
Rig: Schooner
Hull: Steel
Year built: 1985
Home port: Opua, North Island
Flag: New Zealand

168

RARA AVIS

Rara Avis was built similar to a "Thames barge," but instead of its usual spritsails, she was rigged as a three-masted Marconi schooner. She also carries two center-board drop-keels instead of the leeboards associated with barges, which help control stability. She was sold to Father Michel Jaouen and Les Amis de Jeudi-Dimanche Foundation of Paris for 1 franc and now serves as a sail training vessel dedicated to the rehabilitation of young prisoners and drug addicts.

SCANTLINGS
Length overall: 125'
Beam: 23'
Draft: 5' 13"
Hull: Steel
Rig: Marconi schooner
Year built: 1957
Home port: Brest
Flag: France

LA RECOUVRANCE

La Recouvrance is a twentieth-century vessel built on the 1817 plans of an unusual topsail schooner. During the nineteenth-century, when marine warfare in Europe was frequent, the French developed a lightly armed vessel with a hull fast enough to outsail most men-of-war. Used as messengers and to gather intelligence about hostile fleets, these vessels were fast enough to run rather than fight.

Desiring to host a sailing festival in 1992, the City of Brest formed an association to plan and build a ship to represent the city. Research in the archives of the Service Historique de la Marine uncovered plans for a 75-foot naval schooner and work began. The keel was laid in 1991, and the hull was launched during the Brest '92 Sea Festival. Completion of the ship's interior required several more years. Finished in 1996, ownership of *La Recouvrance* was transferred to a semi-public organization in which Brest was the major partner.

Today, *La Recouvrance* serves as an ambassador for Brest at port events, festivals, and races throughout Europe.

SCANTLINGS
Length overall: 138'
Beam: 21'
Draft: 12'
Hull: Wood
Rig: Topsail schooner
Year built: 1992
Home port: Brest
Flag: France

SCANTLINGS
Length overall: 77'
Beam: 17' 6"
Draft: 6' 5"
Hull: Wood
Rig: Gaff topsail schooner
Year built: 1986
Home port: Chicago, Illinois
Flag: United States

RED WITCH

Architect John G. Alden adapted the lines of a typical nineteenth-century gaff-rigged coastal schooner for the plans of the *Red Witch*. Built by Nathaniel Zirlott in Bayou La Batre, Alabama, in 1986, her crimson hull is mahogany over cypress frames and her deck is Douglas fir. *Red Witch* spent her first decade as a charter vessel operating in Pacific waters around Hawaii and off the coast of southern California. The City of Port Clinton, Ohio, then acquired her for sail training programs and to carry visitors on Great Lakes cruises. She was designated a flagship when the State of Ohio celebrated its bicentennial in 2003. She was then acquired by Lakeshore Sail Charters and shifted her home port to Chicago, Illinois, where she is available for regular cruises and charters.

Red Witch is named after the epic sea story *Wake of the Red Witch*, by Garland Roark. John Wayne and Gail Russell starred in the 1949 movie version, and posters promoting the film decorate the boat's saloon.

RETURN of MARCO POLO

Return of Marco Polo is the English sister ship of the Danish sail training schooner *Den Store Bjørn* in form and function. Almost an exact duplicate in her measurements, *Return of Marco Polo* is also a converted Danish lightship.

Built originally in 1906 for lightship service, *Return of Marco Polo* was retired in 1985. In 1990 she was acquired by the Tvind Organization and converted to her present rigging and function in 1993. She is easily identified by the figurehead of her namesake, the famed Venetian explorer and sailor of the thirteenth and fourteenth centuries.

As does her counterpart, this schooner works with youth and the Tvind Organization and is owned by the Small School at Winestead Hall in Hull, England.

SCANTLINGS
Length overall: 143'
Beam: 22'
Draft: 12'
Hull: Wood
Rig: Schooner
Year built: 1907
Home port: Hull, England
Flag: United Kingdom

LE RENARD

This dashing French corsair (the rig is known as a cutter in England) is a replica of similar vessels that protected the French coast during the eighteenth and nineteenth centuries. Built in 1988, *Le Renard,* the fox, sails from St. Mâlo as its representative and as a congenial ambassador to maritime festivals along the northern coast of France.

SCANTLINGS
Length overall: 98'
Beam: 19' 6"
Draft: 9'
Hull: Wood
Rig: Cutter
Year built: 1988
Home port: St. Mâlo
Flag: France

ROALD AMUNDSEN

Named for the Norwegian explorer who was the first man to reach the South Pole, *Roald Amundsun* has a unique history in her own right and is a welcome addition to the tall ship fleet in the North and Baltic Seas.

For years she served as a "tank lugger" on the German coast, was rebuilt as a sailing brig in 1992, and first sailed in 1993. Since that time she has carried crews of sail trainees to European and American ports. *Roald Amundsen* is owned and operated by LebenLernen auf Segleschiffen, eV.

SCANTLINGS
Length overall: 165'
Beam: 23' 6"
Draft: 13' 10"
Hull: Steel
Rig: Brig
Year built: 1992
Home port: Wolgast, Germany
Flag: Germany

ROBERT C. SEAMANS

Upon her dedication at Tacoma, Washington, on June 23, 2001, the *Robert C. Seamans* became the third vessel in the Sea Education Association's fleet of sailing school ships and will join *Corwith Cramer* and *Westward* as platforms for college-level curriculums in oceanography and marine sciences.

Robert C. Seamans is named for the former Secretary of the Air Force, former Deputy Administrator for the National Oceanic and Atmospheric Administration, and longtime board member of the Sea Education Association. The steel-hulled brigantine's plans called for American construction and J.M. Martinac was awarded the contract.

Designed with scientific research a priority, *Robert C. Seamans* is equipped with state-of-the-art laboratories and equipment, as well as the necessary computer support for long-term studies and cruises. The Sea Education Association worked with several west coast institutions, notably the University of Southern California and the University of Washington at Tacoma, to create a variety of undergraduate programs in ecology and marine biology.

SCANTLINGS
Length overall: 134' 6"
Beam: 25' 5"
Draft: 12' 3"
Hull: Steel
Rig: Brigantine
Year built: 2001
Home port: Woods Hole, Massachusetts
Flag: United States

SCANTLINGS
Length overall: 76'
Beam: 11'
Draft: 11'
Hull: Steel
Rig: Staysail schooner
Year built: 1977
Home port: Hamilton,
  Bermuda
Flag: Bermuda

ROCK STEADY

Built in 1977 as a working schooner, *Rock Steady* (until recently, named *Christian Venturer*) originally carried a junk rig with lugsails. Converted in the 1980s to a staysail schooner, she has represented the island of Bermuda at many tall ship events. Designed and owned by William Nash and Richard Doe, *Rock Steady* hosts a variety of sail training and educational programs. This versatile schooner also serves occasionally as a research vessel exploring the waters off the Bermuda coast and in the Gulf Stream. She was sold to a foundation in Bermuda, which is known as The Rock, hence the new name.

SCANTLINGS
Length overall: 137'
Beam: 25'
Draft: 13'
Hull: Wood
Rig: Schooner
Year built: 1925
Home port: Camden, Maine
Flag: United States

ROSEWAY

Until 1975, the *Roseway* was the last pilot schooner still sailing in the United States. She was acquired by the Boston Harbor Pilot Association in 1941 and served for thirty-four years out of Boston harbor. Originally built as a private fishing vessel in 1925, *Roseway* was built of oak at the J. F. James shipyard in Essex, Massachusetts. In 1975, *Roseway* was refitted for the passenger charter trade of coastal Maine and now has fourteen comfortable cabins. A pine tree, the state tree of Maine, decorates her foremast.

ROYAL CLIPPER

Billed as the "largest tall ship in the world," the *Royal Clipper* measures 439 feet from the tip of the bowsprit to the stern. Built as a luxury sailing ship, the five-masted, fully rigged vessel carries more than 90 crew members and has accommodations for 220 passengers on its one- and two-week cruises.

Originally designed to be a large sailing ship for the former Soviet Union in the late 1980s, the hull was built in Gdansk, Poland. After searching for a suitable design, the owner of the *Royal Clipper,* Michael Krafft, decided to adapt his vision of a large tall ship to the hull. The finished hull was moved to Belgium and during the late 1990s, the rig and internal structure was completed.

The *Royal Clipper* began service in the Caribbean and Mediterranean in 1999.

SCANTLINGS
Length overall: 439'
Beam: 54'
Draft: 18' 6"
Hull: Steel
Rig: Fully rigged, five-masted ship
Year built: 1988–2000
Home port: Barbados
Flag: Barbados

TS ROYALIST

Owned by the Sea Cadets Association of Great Britain, this sail training brig was built in 1971. She carries a permanent crew of eight officers and twenty-four cadets on her sail training cruises.

The Sea Cadets are independent of the royal navy, yet they do receive some navy funding. The aim of the Sea Cadets and the *Royalist* is youth development, but not necessarily to make seafarers of the cadets.

Serious fun is the watchword of the Sea Cadets, who are ages thirteen to eighteen, for whom sailing on the *Royalist* provides both a challenge and adventure. For the Sea Cadets, being on the *Royalist* offers a first real taste of the sea. Each cadet takes part in such watch-keeping duties as steering, lookout, sail handling, and navigation. In turn, each also spends time at more mundane chores, like scrubbing the deck, polishing brass, and peeling potatoes. True to nautical tradition, the Sea Cadets observe the raising of "colors" at sunrise and the lowering of colors at sunset. In addition, most cadets can pipe the ceremonial "Bos'n's Call" to greet returning officers and to announce guests of the ship.

SCANTLINGS
Length overall: 97'
Beam: 19'
Draft: 8' 6"
Hull: Steel
Rig: Brig
Year built: 1971
Home port: Portsmouth, England
Flag: United Kingdom

SAGRES II

Sagres II sails under the Portuguese flag as a naval training ship. She was built in 1937 at the Blohm & Voss shipyard in Hamburg, Germany, and is virtually a sister ship to the *Eagle, Mircea, Tovarishch,* and *Gorch Fock II.* Originally named *Albert Leo Schlageter,* she served under American and Brazilian flags before being acquired by Portugal in 1962. At that time she replaced the first *Sagres,* which was built in 1896 as the *Rickmer Rickmers.* The original *Sagres* has now been restored and serves as a museum ship in Hamburg, Germany.

The name *Sagres* derives from the historic port that sent forth many famed Portuguese explorers and navigators. It served as the home and base for Prince Henry the Navigator (1394–1460). His court in Sagres was responsible for the geographic studies and practical explorations that made Portugal master of the seas in the early fifteenth century. A bust of Prince Henry serves as the figurehead on the bow of *Sagres II,* and the ship is easily identified by the traditional Portuguese crosses of Christ (Maltese crosses) that mark the square sails on her fore- and mainmasts.

SCANTLINGS
Length overall: 293' 6"
Beam: 39' 6"
Draft: 17'
Hull: Steel
Rig: Barque
Year built: 1937
Home port: Lisbon
Flag: Portugal

ST. LAWRENCE II

In the early 1950s, the Royal Canadian Sea Cadet Corps in Kingston, Ontario, Canada, was a thriving organization in need of a training vessel. When a suitable boat could not be found, Francis A. MacLachlan and Michael Eames designed *St. Lawrence II*. She was planned to be manageable by a young crew, while offering the complexity and challenge of square-rig sailing.

The nonprofit Brigantine, Inc., was established to fund construction and support of the vessel. The hull was launched in 1953 at the Kingston Shipyard. For the next several years, cadets and volunteers worked to finish her. She sailed first in 1955 and went into full service as a training ship in 1957. She is sailed by a crew of twenty-eight, including eighteen trainees. Trainee slots are open to young people ages thirteen to eighteen years. The captain is usually the only adult aboard.

Each year *St. Lawrence II* sails more than 4,000 miles, spends more than forty nights at sea, and introduces some three hundred trainees to traditional shipboard life on the Great Lakes.

SCANTLINGS
Length overall: 72'
Beam: 15'
Draft: 8' 6"
Hull: Steel
Rig: Brigantine
Year built: 1953
Home port: Kingston, Ontario
Flag: Canada

SEDOV

Sedov is the world's largest tall ship still in service and was one of the last barques built for deepwater cargo carrier service from South America and Australia to the German ports of Bremen and Hamburg. Constructed in 1921 as *Magdalene Vinnen* in Kiel, Germany, she sailed for the Bremen firm of F. A. Vinnen, hence her name. Following the German commercial tradition, she was christened in honor of one of the owner's female family members. After being sold to the shipping conglomerate Norddeutscher Lloyd in 1936, she was renamed *Kommodore Johnson* and served as a sail training vessel. After World War II she was appropriated by the Russian Ministry of Fisheries and was renamed for the Soviet polar explorer and oceanographer Georgij Sedov (1877–1914). *Sedov* is the largest square-rigger still in service from the days of deepwater cargo sailing. She is 10 feet longer than the other giant Russian barque, *Kruzenshtern*.

Besides her physical statistics, such as masts that rise 184 feet above the deck and a length of 386 feet, *Sedov* boasts its own bakery, workshop, and first-aid station. During the tall ship competition of 1992, she also impressed the international fleet with a documented speed of 17 knots in heavy winds. When her thirty-seven sails—covering an area of some 44,000 square feet—fill with a following wind, *Sedov* is a magnificent portrait of sail power.

SCANTLINGS
Length overall: 386'
Beam: 48'
Draft: 27'
Hull: Steel
Rig: Four-masted barque
Year built: 1921
Home port: Murmansk
Flag: Russia

SHABAB of OMAN

Built in Scotland in 1971 as a sail training vessel, *Shabab of Oman* was acquired by the Sultanate of Oman in 1979. *Shabab of Oman,* which means "youth of Oman," serves as a training ship for the royal navy of Oman and also trains young men from other Omani government bureaus.

The sculptured figurehead on her bow is a replica of the fifteenth-century Omani mariner Ahmed bin Majed, who helped the Portuguese sailor Vasco da Gama explore Africa and India. The turban-clad Majed cuts a rakish figure, wearing a green sash and red "khunjar," a traditional dagger. The red coat-of-arms of the sultanate is recognizable on the sails of *Shabab of Oman* and consists of a khunjar superimposed on a pair of crossed scimitars.

SCANTLINGS
Length overall: 171'
Beam: 28'
Draft: 15'
Hull: Wood
Rig: Barquentine
Year built: 1971
Home port: Muscat
Flag: Sultanate of Oman

SHENANDOAH

A graceful ocean cruiser, *Shenandoah* is at home on all seven seas. She was built on Shooters Island in New York Harbor in 1902 as an American luxury yacht. This distinctive three-masted schooner has had American, Danish, English, French, German, Italian, and, now, Japanese owners. Throughout her transitions, however, *Shenandoah* has remained stately, with long, elegant lines. While she was owned by Baron Marcel Bich she returned to the Atlantic coast of the United States, specifically to Newport, Rhode Island, for the French challenge to the 1974 America's Cup. *Shenandoah* combines an elegant profile with luxurious accommodations and is comfortable in Newport or St. Tropez but best under blue skies, in open water, reaching windward.

SCANTLINGS
Length overall: 163'
Beam: 28' 2"
Draft: 15' 6"
Hull: Steel
Rig: Schooner
Year built: 1902
Home port: Bangkok
Flag: Thailand

SCANTLINGS
Length overall: 142'
Beam: 26'
Draft: 14'
Hull: Wood
Rig: Schooner
Year built: 1942
Home port: Boothbay, Maine
Flag: United States

SHERMAN ZWICKER

One of the last wooden schooners built to fish the Grand Banks off Newfoundland, Canada, *Sherman Zwicker* was constructed in 1942 at the Smith and Rhuland Yard in Lunenburg, Nova Scotia. She is owned by the Grand Banks Schooner Museum and spends the summer and fall seasons at the Maine Maritime Museum in Bath, where she is exhibited as a historic vessel. *Sherman Zwicker* continues to be a regular visitor to her home waters in Canada.

SHTANDART

Built as a replica of Peter the Great's original frigate, *Shtandart* recalls St. Petersburg's great maritime history and legacy.

After returning from a voyage to England and Holland in 1968, Peter the Great set to work building the port of St. Petersburg with the knowledge he had acquired overseas. His "window to the West" soon became the center of Russian political and cultural life. The original *Shtandart* was built in 1703 to defend the new capital and was in commission until 1728.

In 1998 the present *Shtandart* was built in anticipation of the 300th anniversary of the St. Petersburg port. The modern frigate was constructed to be as historically accurate as possible in size and appearance.

Shtandart is operated by the Maritime Education Center in St. Petersburg. The organization brings traditional shipbuilding skills to young Russians through voyages with youth groups. The Russian, British, and Dutch governments have all provided support to the project.

SCANTLINGS
Length overall: 113' 2"
Beam: 22' 9"
Draft: 8' 2"
Hull: Wood
Rig: Frigate
Year built: 1999
Home port: St. Petersburg, Russia
Flag: Russia

SIMON BOLIVAR

Simon Bolivar was one of four barques built in Spain for Latin American countries. Similar in design and rigging, the four ships are nearly identical sister ships: *Gloria* from Columbia, *Guayas* from Ecuador, *Cuauhtemoc* from Mexico, and *Simon Bolivar*. All four are frequent visitors to the United States and at major tall ship gatherings.

The 270-foot *Simon Bolivar* was completed in 1980 and named for the "great liberator" of northern South America. Bolivar (1783–1830) was instrumental in the independence of Columbia, Ecuador, Panama, Peru, and Venezuela.

Simon Bolivar embodies the spirit of idealism and freedom of her namesake. Her figurehead is an allegorical depiction of Liberty and was designed by the Venezuelan artist Manuel Felipe Rincon.

SCANTLINGS
Length overall: 270'
Beam: 35'
Draft: 14' 6"
Hull: Steel
Rig: Barque
Year built: 1980
Home port: La Guaira
Flag: Venezuela

SØREN LARSEN

A television star, *Søren Larsen* appeared in the popular BBC series "The Onedin Line" before resuming her more traditional sailing function in the 1st Fleet Reenactment in Australia in 1987 and the Grand Columbus Regatta in 1992, representing New Zealand.

Originally built in Denmark, she was acquired by the Jubilee Sailing Trust in 1983 and has been a part of Square Sail Pacific, which is based in New Zealand, and serves as sail training vessel.

SCANTLINGS
Length overall: 145'
Beam: 25' 6"
Draft: 11' 3"
Hull: Wood
Rig: Brigantine
Year built: 1949
Home port: Auckland, New Zealand
Flag: United Kingdom

SØRLANDET

One of the smallest but more traveled of the full-rigged school ships, *Sørlandet* has had a difficult history since her launch in 1927. Built as a school ship, she was drafted into cargo and transport service and was also used as a storage depot in World War II, when she was heavily damaged. Returned to Norway after the war, she was adopted by the town of Kristiansand, her home port, and has been refurbished for both adventure and educational purposes.

Sørlandet has an exceptional heritage, coming as she does from the days of tall ships and fast clippers. She is now owned and operated by a public foundation, the *Sørlandet* Seilende Skoleskibs Institution, which is controlled and partly funded by the Norwegian Department of Culture. Participation in cruises on *Sørlandet* is open to anyone between the ages of sixteen and seventy-five of either sex and any nationality.

SCANTLINGS
Length overall: 216'
Beam: 29' 6"
Draft: 14' 6"
Hull: Steel
Rig: Full-rigged ship
Year built: 1927
Home port: Kristiansand
Flag: Norway

SOUNDWATERS

This three-masted *sharpie* is a gaff-rigged schooner and the flagship of the environmental organization Soundwaters, which is dedicated to the restoration and preservation of Long Island Sound. Sharpies were first used in the Connecticut oyster fishery industry, and the design spread throughout the eastern seaboard. With very shallow draughts, they were wide-beamed, flat-bottomed, used centerboards, and could be rigged as sloops or schooners.

In addition to sail training, *Soundwaters* sails between ports along Long Island Sound from April 15 to November 15 introducing young people and adults to the ecology of the Sound by reviewing its history and marine science.

SCANTLINGS
Length overall: 80'
Beam: 16'
Draft: 2' 9" (8' 8" lowered centerboard)
Hull: Steel
Rig: Schooner
Year built: 1986
Home port: Stamford, Connecticut
Flag: United States

SPIRIT OF MASSACHUSETTS

The *Spirit of Massachusetts* is a traditionally rigged, wooden, two-masted schooner based on a nineteenth-century design for a Gloucester fishing vessel, the *Fredonia*. The original design, by Edward Burgess, was drawn in 1889 for a "fast and able" vessel to fish the Grand Banks and Georges Banks of the North Atlantic. Like many New England fishing vessels, *Spirit* incorporates design features that ensure speed and versatility as well as resilience in the face of harsh conditions at sea.

Construction of the schooner began in Boston under the auspices of the New England Historic Seaport in 1983, and *Spirit of Massachusetts* was commissioned in 1984. The design uses a wide variety of timber from many regions of the United States. *Spirit* now supports an extensive sail training and youth program in the waters of the U.S. east coast and the Caribbean. Since her launching, *Spirit of Massachusetts* has traveled more than 100,000 miles and has been seen by millions of people. She is a most unusual educational tool and is open to all.

SCANTLINGS
Length overall: 125'
Beam: 24'
Draft: 10'
Hull: Wood
Rig: Schooner
Year built: 1984
Home port: Boston, Massachusetts
Flag: United States

SCANTLINGS
Length overall: 256'
Beam: 34' 5"
Draft: 15' 8"
Hull: Steel
Rig: Ship
Year built: 1998
Home port: Amsterdam
Flag: Netherlands

STAD AMSTERDAM

Clipper ships are the fastest cargo-carrying sailing vessels ever built. On long voyages across the Pacific and Atlantic Oceans, they often average 17–19 knots. Until the transcontinental railroads were established, clippers were the fastest and most economical way to transport cargo.

In the 1840s, the discovery of gold in Australia sparked Dutch interest in the clipper trade. The original *Amsterdam,* on which *Stad Amsterdam* is modeled, was commissioned by the shipping firm of Louis Bienfait & Sons.

Registered in 1854, she was one of the first riveted iron clippers built. Though she missed the California gold rush, between 1854 and 1866, Amsterdam carried cargo between Europe, Australia, and the Dutch East Indies. *Stad Amsterdam* is built in tribute to Dutch maritime history of the nineteenth century and will give its crew and passengers the experience of sailing a true clipper.

STAR OF INDIA

Flagship of the San Diego Maritime Museum fleet, *Star of India* is the oldest active square-rigger in the world. She was designed as a deepwater cargo vessel. Built in 1863 at the Gibson, McDonald & Arnold yard on the Isle of Man, her hull is iron-clad, since her construction predated the use of steel for sailing ships.

Christened *Euterpe* for the Greek goddess of music, she made two accident-plagued voyages to India. She was sold in 1871 to the Shaw Saville & Co. Line in London and circled the globe twenty-one times and faced countless perils without an auxiliary engine. She was sold in 1898 to U.S. owners and again four years later to the Alaska Packers Association, which renamed her *Star of India* and converted her to a floating salmon cannery.

In 1926, a group of idealistic San Diegans paid $9,000, the value of her metal, to save *Star of India* from the scrapper's torch. Unfortunately, the effort to renew *Star of India* languished until the 1950s, when legendary Capt. Alan Villiers prompted the city to show civic pride in its marine heritage. Finally, in 1976, *Star of India* put to sea in San Diego Bay for the first time in fifty years.

A National Historic Landmark, *Star of India* hosts thousands of school children each year, many participating in overnight living-history programs on board. A wide range of cultural events is held on her decks, ranging from chantey festivals to performances of Gilbert and Sullivan operas. Although she is infrequently sailed, there are plans under way that will see *Star of India* put to sea again.

SCANTLINGS
Length overall: 278'
Beam: 35'
Draft: 21' 6"
Hull: Iron
Rig: Barque
Year built: 1863
Home port: San Diego, California
Flag: United States

STATSRAAD LEHMKUHL

Statsraad Lehmkuhl is Norway's largest and oldest square-rigged sailing ship. She is a three-masted barque built in 1914 at the J. C. Tecklenborgwerft yard in Bremerhaven, Germany, as a training ship for the German merchant navy. Originally christened *Grossherzog Fridrich August,* she saw no service during World War I.

In 1923, she was purchased by agents in Bergen for the Norwegian Shipowners Association on the initiative of secretary of state Kristoffer Lehmkuhl. For his work in promoting the cause of cadet ships and for his contributions to the creation of an independent Norwegian government in 1905, the ship was renamed in his honor.

In 1924 the training ship was transferred to the Bergen Schoolship Association, which operated the vessel through difficult years until 1979 under the direction of Hilmar Reksten.

In 1979, the ship was donated to Stiftelsen Seilskipet Statsraad Lehmkuhl, or the *Statsraad Lehmkuhl* Sailing Vessel Foundation. The board of directors of this foundation comprises representatives of national and local governments, the Maritime Museum of Bergen, the firm of Hilmar Reksten, and the city of Bergen. All are committed to restoring and operating the vessel as a cadet ship. Today she carries young people across oceans to discover the romance of the sea and the adventure of sailing.

SCANTLINGS
Length overall: 321' 6"
Beam: 41'
Draft: 17'
Hull: Steel
Rig: Barque
Year built: 1914
Home port: Bergen
Flag: Norway

STAVROS S NIARCHOS

Stavros S Niarchos and her sister brig, *Prince William,* were built by Appledore Shipbuilders in North Devon to replace the sea-weary Sail Training Association schooners *Malcolm Miller* and *Sir Winston Churchill,* both of which have been decommissioned. *Stavros* was designed with the latest sailing developments in mind. She incorporates modern technology to make sail training as accurate as possible.

As part of the Sail Training Association's mission, *Stavros* is dedicated to boosting the self-confidence of young people through the basic operation of the vessel. Students who participate in the ship's voyages are expected to participate in all daily ship duties, from steering and sail trimming to keeping the ship's log.

SCANTLINGS
Length overall: 195'
Beam: 32' 6"
Draft: 14' 8"
Hull: Steel
Rig: Brig
Year built: 2000
Home port: London, England
Flag: United Kingdom

HMS SURPRISE

This ship is a replica of the British frigate HMS *Rose* built in Hull, England, in 1757. HMS *Surprise* (formerly HMS *Rose*) was built in 1970 at the Lunenburg shipyard, Nova Scotia, Canada, from original plans in the National Maritime Museum in Greenwich, England. After several ownership transfers, she was acquired by the HMS Rose Foundation and extensively rebuilt between 1985 and 1991 to bring her into compliance with Sailing School Vessel and U.S. Coast Guard standards and regulations.

She has a displacement of 500 tons and carries 13,000 square feet of sail. Despite looking like a cover model for a Patrick O'Brian novel, the HMS *Surprise* has adapted to the concerns of the present. The same picturesque, billowing sails are technically and environmentally state-of-the-art innovations. They are made of recycled plastic beverage bottles and car fenders. HMS *Surprise*, renamed when it was recently purchased by the San Diego Maritime Museum, has three masts, a flying jib on the bow, a spanker on the stern, and boasts twenty-four cannons.

SCANTLINGS
Length overall: 179'
Beam: 32'
Draft: 13'
Hull: Wood
Rig: Ship
Year built: 1970
Home port: San Diego, California
Flag: United States

SUSAN CONSTANT

Susan Constant is a full-scale replica of the flagship of the three-vessel fleet that brought the first English colonists to the New World in 1607. Built and commissioned on the grounds of the Jamestown Settlement in 1991, *Susan Constant's* design is typical of seventeenth-century vessels of her stated tonnage. She is exhibited at the Jamestown Settlement in Williamsburg, Virginia.

With a crew of staff and volunteers, the *Susan Constant* and her sister replicas, *Godspeed* and *Discovery,* periodically sail to ports in the Chesapeake Bay region to commemorate historical events and anniversaries and to host educational and historical programs.

SCANTLINGS
Length overall: 116'
Beam: 24' 10"
Draft: 11' 6"
Hull: Wood
Rig: Barque (lateen mizzen)
Year built: 1991
Home port: Jamestown, Virginia
Flag: United States

SWAN

The last of her breed, *Swan* is a "Fifie" with vertical stem and stern posts. Typical of nineteenth-century Scottish fishing boats, Fifies were originally about 30 feet long and had open designs, but the need to fish farther offshore led to longer, fully decked designs, lug-rigged with a jib and mizzen.

Built at the start of the twentieth century in Freefield, *Swan* was the finest product in Hay and Company's fleet of Scottish herring luggers. In fact, local experts considered her to be one of the finest fishing boats in northern Scotland at the time. She remained smack-rigged until 1935, when she was one of only five herring sailboats in the Shetlands. In the 1950s she was retired and used as a houseboat. Forty years later, *Swan* was discovered beside a Hartlepool quay and returned to Lerwick in April 1991. Thanks to a group of enthusiasts, she was fully restored over the next few years.

In 1996 *Swan* was relaunched. She has retained many of her original features. A hydraulic capstan has replaced the heavy gear of her original steam rig, however, and the main fish room amidship has been converted to a cabin with 15 berths.

SCANTLINGS
Length overall: 67' 10"
Beam: 60' 4"
Draft: 9'
Hull: Wood
Rig: Smack rig
Year built: 1900
Home port: Lerwick, Shetland Islands
Flag: United Kingdom

SWAN FAN MAKKUM

Majestic and graceful, *Swan Fan Makkum* is distinguished by the five square sails carried on her foremast. Billed as the world's largest brigantine, at an overall length of 203 feet, *Swan Fan Makkum* flies as many as fourteen sails when she sets a course for the Baltic, the North Sea, or, in winter, the Canary Islands and the Caribbean. Operating as a charter vessel, she offers exceptional accommodations in a true windjammer environment.

SCANTLINGS
Length overall: 203'
Beam: 30'
Draft: 12' 3"
Hull: Steel
Rig: Brigantine
Year built: 1993
Home port: Makkum
Flag: Netherlands

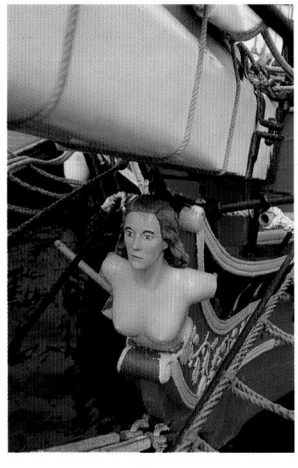

SCANTLINGS
Length overall: 90'
Beam: 18'
Draft: 10'
Hull: Wood
Rig: Square topsail schooner
Year built: 1938
Home port: San Pedro, California
Flag: United States

SWIFT OF IPSWICH

Built at the Ipswich, Massachusetts, yard of William Robinson in 1938, *Swift of Ipswich* was designed on the lines of a Revolutionary War privateer and blockade runner called *Swift*. The size and rig of the original *Swift,* a brig, were modified by designer Howard Chappelle, and the result was a smaller, simpler topsail schooner painted in distinctive Robinson Red, a color unique to her builder.

Swift of Ipswich served on the U.S. east coast but was eventually purchased by brothers William and James Cagney, who moved her to California. There she starred in several films but was ultimately unrigged, moved to an inland lagoon, re-rigged and displayed as a curiosity. Later, in the 1970s, she was returned to open water and served as a California charter boat.

Today *Swift of Ipswich* is operated by the Los Angeles Maritime Institute, the educational affiliate of the Los Angeles Maritime Museum. The vessel is used to teach young trainees both sailing and personal skills that will serve them throughout their lives.

A fast sailer, *Swift of Ipswich* spreads more than 5,000 square feet of sail. Handsomely finished, with a classic profile ideally suited for motion pictures, *Swift of Ipswich* carries a permanent reminder of her original home on the east coast. The seal of the Massachusetts Bay Colony is fastened to her stern.

TABOR BOY

Tabor Academy in Marion, Massachusetts, boasts one of the longest established sail training programs in America. Deepwater sailing education began at the school in 1918 when Capt. John Carlson took students to sea on the *Black Duck,* a 68-foot wooden schooner loaned to the school. In 1925 Tabor purchased its own vessel, and that 88-foot schooner became the first *Tabor Boy.* The current vessel predates the Tabor program. She was built in Holland as a North Sea pilot schooner in 1914 and delivered harbor pilots to arriving ships for 15 years. Reassigned as a Dutch merchant marine school ship, she was renamed *Bestevaer.* Captured by Germany during World War II, she was eventually returned to Holland, where American businessman Ralph Allen purchased her in 1952. Two years later, Mr. Allen gave her to Tabor. Her current captain, James Geil, reports that *Tabor Boy*'s sea-keeping qualities make her ideal for sail training. Built for heavy weather in the North Sea with a short sail plan and long, straight keel, she sails comfortably in heavy weather and can heave-to even in gale-force winds. Although she weighs 160 tons, she handles well underway, can make 200 nautical miles in 24 hours, and tacks efficiently into a harbor.

Despite her more than 90 years, *Tabor Boy* is now a U.S. Coast Guard–inspected and –certificated Sailing School Vessel and carries students on an active schedule of cruises in Atlantic waters of the United States and beyond.

SCANTLINGS
Length overall: 115'
Beam: 21' 8"
Draft: 10' 4"
Rig: Topsail schooner
Hull: Iron
Year built: 1914
Homeport: Marion, Massachusetts
Flag: United States

TALOFA

Talofa in Polynesian means "Queen of the Seas." Charles and Chester Carter built her to look for a ship run aground near the Solomon Islands. They had seen the ship, filled with copper ingots being shipped to the Allied munitions factories, while they were on a military ship during World War I. A fortune hunter's dream was born.

The Carters and others worked on her with limited funds for more than fourteen years but never finished her. World War II began, and she took up valuable space in the shipyard, so she had to be launched without rigging. She became an unfinished "live-aboard" for the aging brothers in the Oakland estuary.

Several owners and many years later, *Talofa* is privately owned and has been completely refitted as a 1930s-era yacht. She is used for eco-tours and adventure cruises but is also a sail training vessel for American Sail Training Association events.

SCANTLINGS
Length overall: 97'
Beam: 18'
Draft: 9'
Hull: Wood
Rig: Square topsail/Marconi
  rigged staysail schooner
Year built: About 1942
Power: Diesel
Home port: Porto Las Cabos,
  Baja California Sur, Mexico
Flag: United States

SCANTLINGS
Length overall: 177'
Beam: 28'
Draft: 13' 9"
Hull: Steel
Rig: Barque
Year built: 1997
Home port: Kochi,
 India
Flag: India

INS TARANGINI

INS *Tarangini*, the first sail training ship in the Indian navy, was commissioned on November 11, 1997, and ports in Kochi on the southwest coast of India. The three-masted barque was designed by British shipwright Colin Mudie.

INS *Tarangini* sails with a permanent complement of six officers and twenty-three sailors and can accommodate up to thirty trainees at a time. Her primary mission is to train cadets for the Indian navy's First Training Squadron. She will also be used to train cadets from the National Defense Academy and the Naval Academy of India.

The name *Tarangini* comes from the Hindi word "tarang," which means "waves." A crest on the ship depicts a mother swan teaching her child to fly and swim, symbolizing the role of the ship in officer training. The swans glide and dance over the waves like a sailing ship at sea, and the spread wings resemble the white sails of the ship from afar.

TENACIOUS

The second of two vessels built by the Jubilee Sailing Trust, *Tenacious* was built from timber with the help of more than 1,100 volunteers. Constructed with a unique, upside-down keel, she is more than 200' in length.

Tenacious has special equipment and rigging to accommodate physically challenged youth. Her hull design was carefully researched and developed over a period of seven years to ensure that trainees of all abilities would be able to participate in the daily operations of a tall ship. Wide passageways and exterior lifts between the decks are just two of the many unique features to be found on this special barque.

Along with the Jubilee Sailing Trust's other vessel, *Lord Nelson, Tenacious* offers sail training to youth of all ages.

Of the 16,000 passengers that the Jubilee Sailing Trust has hosted, more than 6,500 were disabled and nearly 3,000 were in wheelchairs.

SCANTLINGS
Length overall: 213' 3"
Beam: 34' 10"
Draft: 14' 9"
Hull: Wood
Rig: Barque
Year built: 2000
Home port: Southampton, England
Flag: United Kingdom

THALASSA

Built as a modern fishing trawler in 1980, *Thalassa* was severely damaged in a collision off the Dutch island of Texel in 1984. Nearly unsalvageable, her fishing career was over, and she was abandoned. In 1994 her hull was purchased by Capt. Arnold Hylkema and Henk Stallings, who initiated her conversion to sail. She was eventually rigged as a barquentine with fourteen sails and was renamed *Thalassa*. She now serves European waters as a charter vessel and sail training ship, although she spends the winter months in the Caribbean.

SCANTLINGS
Length overall: 157' 6"
Beam: 26' 3"
Draft: 12' 6"
Rig: Barquentine
Hull: Steel
Year built: 1980/1994
Home port: Den Helder
Flag: The Netherlands

THOR HEYERDAHL

Named for the Norwegian explorer and anthropologist Thor Heyerdahl, this low-slung topsail schooner is devoted to cross-cultural exchanges and transoceanic scientific expeditions from its land base in Kiel, Germany.

Thor Heyerdahl is remembered for his 1947 reenactment of two voyages across the Pacific in the *Kon-Tiki,* as well as for his 1969 voyage across the Atlantic to the Caribbean in *Ra.* Both voyages sought to prove the possibility of cultural transmigration in primitive seagoing vessels.

SCANTLINGS
Length overall: 164'
Beam: 21' 6"
Draft: 7' 6"
Hull: Iron
Rig: Topsail schooner
Year built: 1930
Home port: Kiel
Flag: Germany

TOLE MOUR

Designed and built in Seattle, Washington, in 1988, *Tole Mour* served as a floating hospital in the Marshall Islands of the South Pacific under the auspices of the Marimed Foundation of Hawaii. The vessel's name was the winning selection from a contest to name the ship held for school children in the Republic of the Marshall Islands. The name means "gift of life and health" in Marshallese.

Tole Mour was chartered by VisionQuest of Pennsylvania to serve as a residential setting and school for adjudicated youth. In 1994 this 156-foot topsail schooner visited various ports on the Great Lakes and the east coast of the United States. *Tole Mour* has now returned to Honolulu, Hawaii, her home port, to continue providing programs for disadvantaged youth in the islands.

Tole Mour was designed by Ewbank, Brooke, and Associates of Auckland, New Zealand, and is nearly a sister ship of the national sail training ship of New Zealand, *Spirit of New Zealand.*

SCANTLINGS
Length overall: 156'
Beam: 31'
Draft: 13' 6"
Hull: Steel
Rig: Topsail schooner
Year built: 1988
Home port: Honolulu
Flag: United States

SCANTLINGS
Length overall: 263'
Beam: 39'
Draft: 17'
Hull: Steel
Rig: Barque
Year built: 1933
Home port: Wilhelmshaven
Flag: Germany

TOVARISHCH

Tovarishch, originally *Gorch Fock,* was the prototype design for four sailing school ships built in the 1930s at the Hamburg shipyard of Blohm & Voss. Her design was used again for the construction of *Gorch Fock II* in the 1950s.

Tovarishch seems to possess phoenix-like qualities. As *Gorch Fock,* she survived World War II, only to be scuttled in Baltic waters off the German coast in May 1945. After three years, she was raised, refurbished by the Soviet Republic, and assigned to the Black Sea. She began to fly the blue and yellow flag of Ukraine in 1992.

By 1997, inadequate maintenance left her stranded in Britain, where she was deemed unsafe. Efforts there to save her failed, but she was rescued from the scrapyard by a German organization, Tall-Ship Friends.

Tovarishch was eventually transferred to Wilhelmshaven. Extensive renovation and restoration are planned to prepare her for a renewed sail training program in the twenty-first century.

Tovarishch, which means comrade, usually sets 25 sails: 10 square sails and 15 fore-and-aft sails.

TRE KRONOR

Tre Kronor was launched and dedicated by Swedish Crown Princess Victoria on August 27, 2005. The event marked the launch almost exactly 380 years earlier of the first *Tre Kronor.* Built on the location of the Stockholm shipyard where her historic predecessor was constructed, the new *Tre Kronor* was the dream of a host of volunteers and supporters who labored for a decade to bring a sail training brig to Stockholm.

The original *Tre Kronor's* history reaches back to Swedish King Gustavus II Adolphus, who in his war against Poland in 1621 ordered ships to be built at the Stockholm yard. In 1622, *Tre Kronor* was added to the list. Measuring 108 feet by her keel and carrying 30 to 32 guns, she was designed by Dutch shipwright Henrik Hybertson. He also designed the *Vasa,* then the largest and most expensive warship ever constructed for the Swedish navy. *Vasa* was launched in 1625 and delivered to the navy in 1626. On her inaugural sail, she encountered a light breeze and heeled so severely that the sea swamped her gun ports. She sank, taking fifty crew members down. Fortunately, *Tre Kronor* did not suffer the same fate.

SCANTLINGS
Length overall: 115'
Beam: 27'
Draft: 10' 5"
Rig: Brig
Hull: Wood
Year built: 2005
Home port: Stockholm
Flag: Sweden

TREE OF LIFE

Built in Nova Scotia using the latest techniques of a wood-epoxy composite, this gaff-rigged schooner recalls the great schooner building tradition of the Canadian Maritimes. This private yacht, which sails with a crew of five, was originally based in Alexandria, Virginia.

After completing a circumnavigation, former owner Kelly Kellogg sold the schooner and moved on to other projects. John Laramee of Newport, Rhode Island, and his wife Sheri bought the boat with plans to fulfill their lifelong dream of sailing around the world on a six-year cruise.

After extensive interior refitting with Koa timber that had been ordered by Kelly Kellogg on his stopover in Hawaii, John and Sheri departed Newport in the fall of 2001. With a crew of several sail trainees, they sailed around the world until 2005. The ship was sold to another family in early 2006.

SCANTLINGS
Length overall: 93'
Beam: 19'
Draft: 8'
Hull: Wood and epoxy
Rig: Schooner
Year built: 1991
Home port: Vancouver, British Columbia
Flag: United States

URANIA

Urania is the flagship of the Royal Netherlands Naval College. Every executive officer who has graduated from the naval college over the past forty years trained on *Urania*. Generally she sails with three officers, two petty officers, and twelve cadets. She is a very active ship and has thrice been the recipient of the prestigious Cutty Sark Trophy, which is awarded annually to a ship that best demonstrates the spirit of sail training. Her original wishbone rig was modified to her present Bermudian ketch rig in the late 1950s.

SCANTLINGS
Length overall: 78'
Beam: 18'
Draft: 9' 10"
Hull: Steel
Rig: Ketch
Year built: 1928
Home port: Den Helder
Flag: Netherlands

VALBORG

Valborg is a fifty-one-year-old vessel built in Porvoo, Finland, that was restored by Finnish tall ship enthusiasts in 1980. Although classified as a ketch, she retains the broad beam, thick keel, and sturdy construction of a Baltic trader.

Valborg, whose name translates "beautiful girl," works with youth in sail training programs out of her home port of Helsinki, Finland. In addition, she runs a program in collaboration with the Scouts of Finland.

SCANTLINGS
Length overall: 120'
Beam: 23' 6"
Draft: 7' 6"
Rig: Ketch
Hull: Wood
Year built: 1948
Home port, Helsinki,
  Finland
Flag: Finland

SCANTLINGS
Length overall: 170'
Beam: 25'
Draft: 7' 5"
Hull: Wood
Rig: Schooner
Year built: 1900
Home port: Rockland,
   Maine
Flag: United States

VICTORY CHIMES

More than a century ago, *Edwin and Maud* slid down the ways at the yard of Phillips & Co., in Bethel, Delaware, to begin her remarkable sailing career. Built of Georgia pine, live oak, and Delaware oak, she was designed to carry lumber up and down the shallow bays and rivers of the Chesapeake Bay. After working on the water for over fifty years, *Edwin and Maud* sailed to Maine to join the fleet of Maine windjammers, where she was rechristened *Victory Chimes*.

Purchased by Domino's Pizza in 1988, she underwent a major refurbishing. In 1990 she was acquired by her present owners and managers, Capt. Kip Files and Capt. Paul DeGaeta, and operates as a charter vessel in Rockland, Maine.

At 208 gross tons, *Victory Chimes* is the largest commercial sailing vessel operating under the U.S. flag. She is also the only original three-master still working in the United States. Recently nominated for status as a National Historic Landmark, *Victory Chimes* seems poised to continue her successful, independent course for another century.

SCANTLINGS
Length overall: 101'
Beam: 19'
Draft: 8' 9"
Rig: Brixham trawler
Hull: Steel
Year built: 1926; rebuilt 1995
Home port: Brixham, Devon
Flag: United Kingdom

VIGILANCE

Built at a Brixham yard in Devon, England, in 1926, Vigilance has enjoyed a varied career. She first sailed with the local fishing fleet and then saw war service as a barrage balloon mooring vessel during World War II. Thereafter, she served as a private yacht, a charter boat, and a sail training vessel in France, Denmark, Ireland, and the Isle of Man.

Sold to Ken Harris in 1980, *Vigilance* received a long-overdue restoration and participated in several Cutty Sark Tall Ships Races, including the events in 1983 when she was sailed by an all-female crew.

In 1997, she was purchased by a group of volunteers and returned to her home port of Brixham. She now sails as a charter boat, and participates in sail training events in the waters off Torbay. As Roger Churchill reports, *Vigilance* sails to one of the tall ship festivals in Brest, Paimpol, or Douarnenez, France, at least once a season. Her colorful sails and the British mooring marks "BM 76" on her mainsail make *Vigilance* is easy to identify in the tall ship fleet.

WESTWARD

Built in 1961 as a private yacht for around the world service, *Westward* shows the graceful lines of a North Sea pilot schooner and is similar in design to Irving Johnson's sail-trainer, *Yankee*.

After thirty years sailing with the Sea Education Alliance of Woods Hole, Massachusetts, *Westward* was purchased for the sea education program of the Ocean Classroom Foundation. After a complete refit, she now offers accredited sailing programs for students.

Westward sails the waters of the western North Atlantic and the Caribbean Sea from Newfoundland to South America. She joins *Harvey Gamage* and *Spirit of Massachusetts* as the third member of the Ocean Classroom fleet. The foundation offers programs for middle school, high school, and college students and at-risk youth. These programs are available to young people from around the United States.

SCANTLINGS
Length overall: 125'
Beam: 22'
Draft: 12'
Hull: Steel
Rig: Schooner
Year built: 1961
Home port: Rockland, Maine
Flag: United States

SCANTLINGS
Length overall: 70'
Beam: 14'
Draft: 6'
Hull: Wood
Rig: Gaff schooner
Year built: 1963
Home port: Abaco
Flag: Bahamas

WILLIAM H. ALBURY

Built by the legendary Bahamian boat builder William H. Albury, this vessel and others of its design are now recognized as Bahamian schooners. *William H. Albury* is a familiar sight among the islands and cays of this beautiful country. William Albury built more than three hundred vessels, most on Man o' War Cay; this 70-foot schooner was his last. Operated by Capt. Joseph Maggio, *William H. Albury* offers a series of scuba and sea exploration programs from Marsh Harbour on Great Abaco Island. *William H. Albury* has represented the Bahamas in several international gatherings of tall ships sponsored by Operation Sail.

YOUNG ENDEAVOUR

Given by the United Kingdom to the government and people of Australia in celebration of that country's bicentenary, *Young Endeavour* serves as Australia's national sail training vessel. She was dedicated with the words of Prime Minister Robert Hawke, "This ship—*Young Endeavour*—bears a name imperishably linked with Captain Cook's great voyage of discovery. And the name itself expresses a great deal of our aspirations for our country." For a land surrounded by the sea, this brigantine is a reminder of the country's maritime heritage. *Young Endeavour*'s arrival in Sydney also heralded the start of a new era of sail training in Australia.

Another Australian link of interest to the world of sail training and tall ships is the pioneering spirit of Capt. Alan Villiers, an Australian born in Melbourne in 1903. In 1934, Captain Villiers purchased *Georg Stage,* renamed her *Joseph Conrad,* and logged over 58,000 miles, advocating ocean adventure and the discipline of sail training as educational goals. His ideas inspired and influenced the founders of England's Sail Training Association and, later, the American Sail Training Association.

Young Endeavour sails with a permanent crew of nine from the Royal Australian Navy and hosts a coeducational crew of twenty-four young people. Each year *Young Endeavour* provides hundreds of youngsters with the opportunity to participate in one of twenty ten-day voyages off the Australian coast.

SCANTLINGS
Length overall: 144' 6"
Beam: 25' 6"
Draft: 13'
Hull: Steel
Rig: Brigantine
Year built: 1987
Home port: Sydney
Flag: Australia

SCANTLINGS
Length overall: 141'
Beam: 22' 3"
Draft: 15'
Hull: Steel
Rig: Schooner
Year built: 1952
Home port: Gdansk
Flag: Poland

ZAWISZA CZARNY

This distinctive schooner, with its unusual wishbone rig, is the flagship of the Polish Pathfinders Union, the Polish version of Sea Scouts. *Zawisza Czarny* was named for the legendary hero of the battle of Grunwald in 1404. One of the last great medieval battles in Poland, Grunwald saw Polish knights under the leadership of Wladislav IV defeat an army of Teutonic knights, thus saving eastern Europe from their dominance. This vessel carries a figurehead of her namesake on her bow and a graphic logo on her square-foresail as reminders to young trainees of the ideals of reliability, courage, and duty embodied by *Czarny's* legacy.

Zawisza Czarny has participated in many festivals, races, and gatherings of tall ships and is a favorite with other crews in the ports she visits. She is noted for her hospitable nightly folk music gatherings and sing-alongs.

The present vessel is the second to be named for Czarny. The original *Zawisza Czarny* was a staysail schooner that served until the outbreak of World War II. Owing to deterioration she was scrapped in 1946. In 1952 reconstruction on a fishing trawler—the current *Zawisza Czarny*—was begun at the Stocznia Polnocna shipyard in Gdansk. Major overhauls in 1965, 1968, and 1980 resulted in her present arrangement, which includes a ballasted keel, three steel masts, and an extended stern.

Her unusual rig, with three staysails set in front of the fore-, main-, and mizzenmasts, carries a complement of eleven sails with a total area of 6,000 square feet. In addition to staysails, she carries a square-foresail before the wind as well as a raffe, which is a small, triangular sail that is hung from the top of mast and secured to the yard below.

ZEELANDIA

This three-masted Dutch schooner is notable for her small, curved bow, rounded counter stern, and extremely shallow draft. Requiring little water under her keel makes *Zeelandia* handy on the inland waterways of The Netherlands. Referred to as a "klipper," the term describes *Zeelandia's* function, not rig. Dutch klippers appeared at the turn of the century and were the steel-hulled equivalent of the American coasting schooner. They were maneuverable in shallow waters, but also capable of transporting large and heavy cargo. Rigged first as single-masted sloops with exaggerated booms, klippers later stepped two or three masts. *Zeelandia* was converted from a cargo carrier to her present rig as a sail training schooner.

SCANTLINGS
Length Overall: 128' 6"
Beam: 17'
Draft: 3' 6"
Hull: Steel
Rig: Schooner
Year built: 1931
Home port: Leeuwarden
Flag: The Netherlands

ZENOBE GRAMME

Serving first as a coastal survey ship, *Zenobe Gramme* is now used as a training ship for the Belgian navy. She is a frequent participant in sail training races and gatherings. Before the wind *Zenobe Gramme* is easily recognized when she sets her spinnaker, which displays the Belgian royal coat-of-arms. *Zenobe Gramme* is named for the Belgian inventor who perfected the technology for alternating-current motors and generators in the 1860s and 1870s.

SCANTLINGS
Length overall: 93'
Beam: 22' 6"
Draft: 8' 6"
Hull: Wood
Rig: Bermuda ketch
Year built: 1961
Home port: Zeebrugge
Flag: Belgium

SCANTLINGS
Length overall: 160'
Beam: 25' 6"
Draft: 16'
Hull: Wood
Rig: Gaff Schooner
Year built: 1924
Home port: Seattle,
  Washington
Flag: United States

ZODIAC

Designed by William H. Hand, Jr., to incorporate the best features of traditional gaff-rigged American fishing schooners, *Zodiac* was built in 1924 at the Hodgdon Brothers Shipyard in East Boothbay, Maine. Owned by heirs of the Johnson and Johnson Company, *Zodiac* sailed as a private yacht. In 1928 she competed in the Transatlantic Race, where light winds led to her late finish.

During the Depression, she was sold to the San Francisco Bar Pilots and renamed *California*. She spent forty years working on the waters off the Golden Gate. When *California* retired in 1972, she was the last working pilot schooner in America.

A nonprofit organization, the Vessel Zodiac Corporation, was formed in the late 1970s to refurbish, operate, and maintain the schooner. Renamed *Zodiac,* she now sails the waters of Puget Sound offering a range of programs from sail training for young people to Elderhostel cruises, in addition to day sails, overnight excursions, and charters.

MARITIME MUSEUMS

AUSTRALIA

Australian National Maritime Museum
Darling Harbor
GPO Box 5131, Sydney
New South Wales 2001

Queensland Maritime Museum
P.O. Box 197
Hamilton
Queensland 4007

South Australian Maritime Museum
135 St. Vincent St.
Post Adelaide
South Australia 5015

Tasmanian Maritime Museum
Secheron House, Battery Point
Hobart 7001

Western Australian Maritime Museum
(home to STS *Leeuwin*; artifacts of *Batavia*)
Old Commiserat Building
Cliff Street
Freemantle 6160

CANADA

Maritime Museum of the Atlantic
1675 Lower Water Street
Halifax, Nova Scotia B3J 153

Maritime Museum of British Columbia
28 Bastion Square
Victoria, British Columbia V8W 1H9

Marine Museum of the Great Lakes
55 Ontario Street
Kingston, Ontario K7L 2Y2

Vancouver Maritime Museum
1905 Ogden Avenue
Vancouver, British Columbia V6J 1A3

FINLAND

Stiftelsen Ålands Sjöfartsmuseum
Hamngaten 2 – PB 98
Mariehamn 22101

GERMANY

Deutschen Schiffahrtsmuseum
(home to *Seute Derne*)
Columbus Center
Bremerhaven

Schiffahrtsmuseum Rostock
Im Steinor
August-Bebel-Strasse 1
D–18055 Rostock, Germany

HOLLAND

Scheepvaartmuseum
(home to *Amsterdam* and *Batavia*)
Kattenburgerplein 1
Amsterdam 1018 KK

Holland Glorie
(home to *Europa, Österschelde, Antigua*)
Industrieweg 135
3044 As Rotterdam

UNITED STATES

CALIFORNIA
Nautical Heritage Museum
(home to *Californian*)
24532 Del Prado
Dana Point, California 92629

San Diego Maritime Museum
(home to *Star of India* and *Star Pilot*)
1386 North Harbor Drive
San Diego, California 92101

San Francisco Maritime National Historic Park
(home to *Alma, Balclutha,* and *C.A. Thayer*)
2905 Hyde Street
San Francisco, California 94109

CONNECTICUT
Aquaculture Foundation and Maritime Center
(home to HMS *Rose* and *Black Pearl*)
Captain's Cover
1 Bostwick Avenue
Bridgeport, Connecticut 06605

Mystic Seaport and Museum
(home to *Joseph Conrad, L. A. Dutton, Charles W. Morgan*)
75 Greenmanville Avenue
Mystic, Connecticut 06355

FLORIDA
Apalachicola Maritime Museum
P.O. Box 625
Apalachicola, Florida 32329

HAWAII
Hawaii Maritime Center
(home to *Falls of Clyde*)
Pier 7
Honolulu, Hawaii 96813

MAINE
Maine Maritime Museum
(home to *Sherman Zwicker*)
243 Washington Street
Bath, Maine 04532

MARYLAND
Chesapeake Bay Maritime Musuem
Navy Point
St. Michael's, Maryland 21663

MASSACHUSETTS
Boston National Historical Park
(home to the USS *Constitution*)
Charlestown Navy Yard
Charlestown, Massachusetts 02129

New England Historic Seaport
(home to *Spirit of Massachusetts*)
Pier 3
Charlestown Navy Yard
Charlestown, Massachusetts 02129

Peabody Essex Musuem
East India Square
Salem, Massachusetts 01970

Salem Maritime National Historic Site
174 Derby Street
Salem, Massachusetts 01970

Sea Education Association
(home to *Corwith Cramer* and *Westward*)
P.O. Box 6
Woods Hole, Massachusetts 02543

MICHIGAN
Michigan Maritime Museum
Dyckman Avenue
South Haven, Michigan 49090

Traverse Tall Ship Company
(home to *Malabar* and *Manitou*)
13390 South West Bay Shore Drive
Traverse City, Michigan 49684

MISSISSIPPI
Maritime and Seafood Industry Museum
(home to *Glenn L. Swetman* and *Mike Sekul*)
P.O. Box 1907
Biloxi, Mississippi 39533

NEW JERSEY
Delaware Bay Schooner Project
P.O. Box 57
Dorchester, New Jersey 08316

NEW YORK
Buffalo Maritime Society
(home to *Sea Lion*)
90 Liberty Terrace
Buffalo, New York 14215

East End Seaport and Marine Foundation
(home to *Regina Maris*)
1 Bootleg Alley
Greenport, New York 11944

Hudson River Maritime Center
1 Rondout Landing
Kingston, New York 12401

South Street Seaport
(home to *Wavertree, Peking, Pioneer,*
and *Lettie Howard*)
207 Front Street
New York, New York 10038

NORTH CAROLINA
North Carolina Maritime Museum
315 Front Street
Beaufort, North Carolina 28516

Southport Maritime Museum
116 North Howe Street
Southport, North Carolina 28461

OHIO
Maritime Museum at Put-in-Bay
Put-in-Bay, Ohio 43456

Inland Seas Maritime Musuem
Great Lakes Historical Society
480 Main Street
Vermillion, Ohio 44089

Great Lakes Historical Society
Inland Seas Maritime Museum
420 Main Street
P.O. Box 435
Vermilion, Ohio 44089–0435

OREGON
Oregon Maritime Center and Musuem
113 Southwest Front Avenue
Portland, Oregon 97204

PENNSYLVANIA
The Flagship *Niagara*
Pennsylvania Historical and
Museum Commission
(home to *Niagara*)
164 East Front Street
Erie, Pennsylvania 16502

Independence Seaport Museum
211 South Columbus Boulevard
Philadelphia, Pennsylvania 19106

RHODE ISLAND
International Yacht Restoration School
(home to *Coronet*)
28 Church Street
Newport, Rhode Island 02640

Museum of Yachting
Fort Adams
P.O. Box 129
Newport, Rhode Island 02840

TEXAS
Texas Seaport Musuem
2016 Strand
Galveston, Texas 77550

VIRGINIA
Nauticus National Maritime Center
1 Waterside Drive
Norfolk, Virginia 23510

Mariners Museum
100 Museum Drive
Newport News, Virginia 23606

WASHINGTON
Gray's Harbor and Historical Seaport
(home to *Lady Washington*)
813 East Heron Street
Aberdeen, Washington 98520

WISCONSIN
Milwaukee Maritime Center
500 North Harbor Drive
Milwaukee, Wisconsin 53202

Wisconsin Maritime Museum
75 Maritime Drive
Manitoc, Wisconsin 54220

GLOSSARY

barque a vessel of three or more masts, all square-rigged except the mast nearest the stern, which is fore-and-aft rigged

barquentine a vessel of three or more masts only the foremost of which is square-rigged; the others are rigged fore-and-aft

beam the measurement of a vessel at its maximum width

Bermuda sail a tall, triangular, fore-and-aft rigged sail that originated on small boats around Bermuda

bisquine a two-masted fishing boat of traditional French design rigged with lug sails

boom a spar to which the foot of a sail is set

bow the foremost part of a vessel

bowsprit a spar extending over the bow of a vessel to which the foremast is secured by means of a forestay; a jib sail can be set from the forestay

brig a two-masted vessel, both masts rigged with square sails and carrying a fore-and-aft rigged sail on the stern side of the main mast

brigantine a two-masted vessel similar to a brig but omitting the large "course," or square sail, on the main mast

capstan a barrel-like device around which a ship's line is wound to lift heavy objects such as an anchor; traditionally powered by crew members pushing on wooden bars

caravel a vessel sailed widely on the Mediterranean by the Portuguese and Spanish between the fourteenth and seventeeth centuries; at first lateen-rigged *(caravela latina),* also rigged with square sails *(caravela rotunda);* Columbus's *Nina* began her voyage to the Americas as a *caravela latina*

centerboard a device lowered from the center of a shallow-draught vessel that resists the sideways pressure of the wind and, in doing so, creates a forward movement

chine point where the bottom and sides of a vessel intersect; when the angle at that point is pronounced, the boat is said to have a hard chine

clipper any one of a number of fast sailing ships; the first vessels so described were Baltimore clippers that were actually rigged as schooners; later designs altered the rig, but in general clippers had hulls deeper aft than forward, sharply raked masts, an overhanging stern, and carried more sail than other ships of comparable size

draft (also **draught**) the measurement between the waterline and the keel; a shallow-draught vessel draws little water

figurehead a carved figure on the bow of a vessel that reflects its name or function

foot the bottom edge of a triangular or square sail

fore-and-aft rigged a vessel with sails set parallel to the length of the vessel

full-rigged a ship of at least three masts, each fitted with a topmast, topgallant mast, and royal mast, all rigged with yards and square sails

gaff a spar laced to the head of a four-sided, fore-and-aft sail used to hoist and set the sail

gaff-rigged a vessel with four-sided, fore-and-aft sails; the head of each sail is laced to a gaff that extends aft of the mast and parallel to the boom to which the sail's foot is laced

galleass designed originally as a warship, this vessel was used during fifteenth- and sixteenth-century naval engagements; armed with a ram, it was powered by both sails and banks of oars; by the seventeeth century, the galleass had evolved to a three-masted lateen-rigged vessel with one bank of oars

gybe (or **jibe**) to change the course or direction of a vessel while keeping the wind across the stern

head the top edge of a four-sided sail

hull the body of a vessel

jib a triangular sail set on a stay or line running from the foremast to the bowsprit or bow; traditional ships carried as many as six jibs

junk the name applied to Far Eastern sailing vessels characterized by flat bottoms, square bows, and high sterns rigged with lug sails and stiffened horizontally by battens

keel the backbone of a ship's hull to which the stem, stern, and hull framing are attached

ketch a two-masted fore-and-aft rigged vessel; the second, or mizzenmast, is shorter than the mainmast and is stepped ahead of the steering position

knot the nautical measure of speed; 1 nautical mile equals 6,080 feet

lateen sail a triangular sail set on a yard (q.v.) that raises the sail and then hangs at about a 45-degree angle to the mast; the foot of the sail is not lashed to a boom

leeboard a device lowered from the side of a shallow-draught vessel that resists the sideways pressure of the wind and in doing so creates a forward movement

length overall the measurement of a vessel from the foremost part of the stempost to the aftermost part of the stern

luff the leading or front edge of a fore-and-aft sail

lug sail a four-sided, fore-and-aft sail narrower at its head than its foot that hangs from a lug or gaff which extends both fore and aft of the mast on which it is hoisted

mainmast the largest mast on a ship

mainsail a vessel's principal sail; on a square-rigged ship, the bottommost and largest sail on the mainmast

mast a vertical spar from which sails are set

mizzenmast the mast nearest the stern of a vessel with three masts; the aftermast of a ketch or yawl

raffe a triangular sail hung from the stays at the top of a mast to the yard of a square sail below; set in light winds, it is also known as a moonraker

rake the degree of angle away from perpendicular at which a mast is set

rig a vessel's arrangement of masts and sails

schooner a two-masted fore-and-aft rigged vessel with the foremast shorter than the mainmast and originally built in the 1700s at Gloucester, Massachusetts; a familiar variation is the fore-and-aft schooner, which carries from two to seven masts, all of equal height, rigged fore-and-aft with topsails, although there are many variations

sheer the curve of a vessel's deck from bow to stern

ship-rigged a vessel with three masts, all carrying square sails and a bowsprit

square-rigged a vessel that carries sails hung from yards that are "square," or perpendicular, to the mast

square sail a four-sided sail that hangs from a yard set "square," or perpendicular, to a mast

staysail a sail, usually triangular, set from a stay or line that supports a mast

stem the foremost hull timber, joined to the keel and to which the planking of the hull is fastened to form the bow of the vessel

stern the rear, or afterend, of a vessel

tack to change the course of a vessel by bringing the bow through the wind

tanbark a traditional method of tanning or treating sails and lines made of cotton or flax to protect them against mildew and rot; changes the color of the sail to a medium brown

thonier a ketch-rigged fishing vessel typical of the French province of Brittany

yard a wood or metal spar from which sails are hung; in square-rigged vessels the yard is set perpendicular to the mast and in lateen-rigged vessels the yard crosses the mast diagonally

yardarm either end of the yard of a square-rigged ship

yawl a two-masted fore-and-aft rigged vessel; the second, or mizzenmast, is shorter than the mainmast and is stepped behind the steering position

BIBLIOGRAPHY

American Sail Training Association
Directory of Sail Training Programs and Tall Ships
Newport, Rhode Island: ASTA, 1998

Bishop, Paul
Tall Ships and the Cutty Sark Races
Henley, England: Aidan Ellis, 1994

Blackburn, Graham
*The Illustrated Encyclopedia of Ships, Boats,
Vessels, and Other Water-borne Craft*
Woodstock, New York: Overlook Press, 1978

Bygholm, Henrik, Peter Haagen, and
Carl Aage Kirkegaard
For Fulde Sejl-Skibe omkring et Sail Training Race
Frederickshavn, Denmark: Bygholm, 1981

Crothers, William L.
The American-built Clipper Ship, 1850–1856
Camden, Maine: International Marine, 2000

Czasnojc, Marek
Swiat Wielkich Zagli
Szczecin, Poland: GLOB JV, 1991

de Kerchove, René
International Maritime Dictionary
New York: Van Norstand Reinhold, 1961

Drumm, Russell
The Barque of Saviors: Eagle's *Passage from
the Nazi Navy to the U.S. Coast Guard*
Boston: Houghton Mifflin, 2001

Gotved, Arne
Og de sejler de gamle traeskibe
Stenstrup, Denmark: Skip Forlag, 2000

Hamilton, John
Sail Training: The Message of the Tall Ships
Northamptonshire, England: Patrick Stephens, 1988

Hollins, Holly
The Tall Ships Are Sailing
London: David & Charles, 1982

Kåhre, Georg
*The Last Tall Ships: Gustav Erikson and
the Ål and Sailing Fleets 1872–1947*
New York: Mayflower Books, 1977

Liberman, Cy and Pat
The Mystique of Tall Ships
Wilmington, Delaware: Middle Atlantic Press, 1986

Lund, Kaj
Sejler I Sigte ! Sail Ho !
Copehagen: Borgen Forlag, 1986

Lund, Kaj
Vinden er vor, Vols. 4 and 5
Tryk, Denmark: Narayana Books, Vol. 4, 1981;
Vol. 5, 1982

Puget, Ollivier
Windjammer der Welt
Hamburg, Germany: Edition Maritim, 1999

SAIL BREMERHAVEN '95
Bremerhaven, Germany:
Tourismus-Förderungsgesellschaft, 1995

SAIL HAMBURG '89
Kurt Grobecker and Illa Schütte, eds.
Hamburg, Germany: Die Barque, 1989

Schäuffelen, Otmar
Die letzen großen Segelschiffe
Bielefeld, Germany: Delius Klasing, 1994

Segelschulschiffe
Norderstedt, Germany: Verlag Egon Heinemann, 1977

INDEX